THE BEANSTALK BOOK

A Magical Guide to Realistically Living Your Enchanted Life

KIM NUSSBAUM HOWERTON

PRAISE FOR KIM NUSSBAUM HOWERTON

The Beanstalk Book: A Magical Guide to Realistically Living Your Enchanted Life is a literal magic-maker.

Kim created a profound path to live her dream life and help others be able to do that too. The extremely effective processes and exuberant art in these pages will inspire and guide you in transforming experiences of pain, grief, trauma, heartbreak and even death, and show you how to bring your dearest dreams to life no matter what your circumstances might be.

SARK, Author, Artist at PlanetSARK.com

Kim, as I read your book, I cannot help but cry when you speak to me as if I am seeing and hearing my own thoughts. With each page, I find commonalities not only you and I share but that most women share when losing their love, their soul mate, their everything. Your writing and imagery are exceptional: the "magical beanstalks" encourage thinking through situations and decisions, deciphering possibilities not imagined when learning to cope with and some day "enjoy alone".

Dr. Sue Clifton, Author at Wild Rose Press

The time I spend "Beanstalking" has allowed for both reflection and projection. I have been able to creatively set a course for my journey into the next chapter of my life. Through Kim's beautiful and imaginative creation, The Beanstalk Book, and with her guidance, I am feeling a sense of joy and peacefulness that is new and so very welcome. Kim's bravery in sharing her own painful journey and her willingness to let us join her as she manifests the life she's dreamed of, has been invaluable in allowing me to believe in myself again. Kim provides a road map for hope, freedom, possibility and a joyful life. And, on top of all that, "Beanstalking" is just a whole lotta fun!!"

Reader Review

Kim helped me to follow my heart and open my own business. Thank you, times a million! She made my dreams, that seemed BIG and unrealistic, on-level and achievable. She moved clouds and paved a way toward sunshine.

Reader Review

Kim's book is a bit whimsical and carefree but tackles tough emotions and real life situations. Her methods for growing and improving are simple and straightforward. She approaches others with kindness, love and tenderness and is always encouraging. She is sensitive and funny and she just sort of sparkles.

Reader Review

DEDICATION

This book is dedicated to the most kind and loving soul on Earth—the dog that I gave as a gift to my husband and who, nine months later, became the dog that rescued me. He was with me through all of the times I thought I would die. He loved me, kissed away my tears, and cared for me when I couldn't do it for myself. He would probably rather we go for a ride in the Jeep than have a book dedicated to him, but I will do both. He saved me. He is my angel on Earth. I can never repay him. Thank you, Boone Dog

CONTENTS

INTRODUCTION

The following pages take you through my journey. I hope the lessons I learned can help you on yours.

I am a girl who thought life was over, but instead of giving up I dared to dream, I created a book to hold those dreams, and magic started happening...and I want that magic to happen for you too.

Once upon a time...

I dreamed of a beautiful porch, cut this picture out of a magazine, and placed it in my dream book.

I now relax on this porch every day. It's not the same porch, but looks like it could be.

I cut this picture of a random man playing guitar out of a magazine.

I am now married to this real life guitar-playing man.

I dreamed of being a writer. I quit my day job and have written and illustrated two books so far.

I put my wishes onto the pages of a book. A book of dreams that I never intended for anyone but me to see… ever. I know now that sharing it can *offer inspiration and healing to others*…which, by the way, are words directly out of my dream book. So I now give you a glimpse into it along with this simple question:

What do you desire?

CHAPTER **ONE**:
WHY THE BEANSTALK BOOK?

This is the story of how, through heartbreak, tears, glimpses of light and a little magic, *The Beanstalk Book* came to be, and how it might come to be in your life.

I was a happy wife with a happy life.

I was with my sweetheart whom I had met when I was in middle school, when my brother brought his new college buddies home for a visit. Years later, when I was 18, I began dating one of those college buddies. We were together for 31 years (married for almost 25). We raised our two beautiful daughters and were planning our future together—a future of exploring, finally having time for each other, retirement, growing old in rocking chairs while holding hands—you know, the whole *happily ever after* thing.

Take a moment here to bask in the beauty of a life where you have everything you ever dreamed of, and now you also have the time and money to relax and actually enjoy it—then imagine it disappears in an instant.

At age 53, my husband, Wesley "Wes," was diagnosed with glioblastoma, a highly aggressive brain cancer. He died 38 days later. Everything I had ever dreamed my life would be was suddenly gone. I was no longer a wife. That happy life—gone.

This is an excerpt from my journal from that time. I don't remember drawing this, but it hit me hard when I later found it.

I was a heap of a human. I was curled up all alone (even when surrounded by people). I cried tears that came all the way from my toes. Sometimes I would resist crying because I thought if I started I wasn't sure if the stream of tears would ever stop. I now think of a cartoon image like how Pigpen from *Peanuts* carried his visible stink around with him. I thought I would have constant tears squirting out wherever I went from then on. The tears eventually stopped (and started and stopped some more and still do), but the pain became more manageable as I grew.

I was always on the lookout for heart-shaped rocks. Wes came home with the middle rock for me one day. I loved that he found one and thought of me. Years later, when he was sick I found the brown rock and gave it to him. After he passed away, my lifelong friend's 11-year-old daughter found the broken-heart rock and asked her mom if she thought I would like it. This is my favorite painting I have ever done.

After Wes died, I was left to live without him and to rediscover me. *Who am I now that "we" are no longer?* No longer Kim and Wes—oof—I can feel the gut punch still. We had been so together—for so long. It was like it was one word KimandWes. Suddenly being just Kim was a daunting task. *Who is Kim? Is she even a whole person without Wes? Is she still worthy of being around, taking up space and breathing air?*

For my whole life I was someone's daughter (the coach's kid), someone's sister (of my older, athlete brothers), and finally I was Wes' wife and my children's mommy. I have always and will always love being their mother. With my children off at college and pursuing their dreams, I enjoyed being Wes' wife and a teacher. I hadn't realized it until he was gone that I have never really been just Kim. *Who is this human called Kim?* I set out on a new journey to rediscover myself and learn to love and appreciate her.

I worked at the most wonderful school with a caring and understanding staff and administration who supported me and allowed me to take a sabbatical from my teaching job. I was teaching first grade at the time. During my time away from teaching, I began my soul journey. I remember sitting on the floor surrounded by hundreds of scattered pictures of a life that I didn't want to admit or accept no longer existed. I looked at all of it. Stared it straight in the face, through blurry vision from tear-filled eyes. I transported myself into each happy scene and reexperienced all of the memories—and then fell apart into a blubbering heap on the floor—and I repeated that a thousand times.

I threw everything at my grief: church-sponsored grief support, psychotherapy, listening to every book about heaven and the afterlife I could get my hands on (I listened, not read, because I had become physically unable to read and comprehend whole pages of text). I prayed like crazy, did Reiki healing, crystals, psychic mediums, meditation, yoga, journaling, napping, and sought out words that inspired me to move forward. I sat alone.

Much of that was during the COVID lockdown, so I was generally isolated, completely alone—just me, my dogs, and my grief. My daughters and I were not near each other during that time because they were living their young adult lives elsewhere. Being alone was difficult, but I knew that I didn't want my grief and theirs to co-mingle. I did not want them taking on my pain, as they had plenty of their own. I also knew that I could not cope with their grief on top of mine. In hindsight, I wish I could have been there for them more. We always, as a family, dealt with hard things together. It may have been by design that I was alone during that time though.

I needed to rediscover me to heal me. In my search for answers I read (listened to) a book called *Signs* by Laura Lynn Jackson, a psychic medium, that changed my course forever. After reading her book I began seeing signs from Heaven everywhere and recognizing times when I had seen them, but had not acknowledged or understood them to be signs.

I saw the number 22 everywhere. I associate 2's with my husband. He was born on December 22 and his last day on Earth was October 22 so it seems serendipitous that I found a workshop held on February 22 that cost $222. Who cared that it was in New York and a ridiculous idea to go?

I asked a friend to join me and she eagerly jumped at the chance to attend the workshop and to see her son who lived in Brooklyn. We lived in Montana, but we swiftly booked our flights to New York to attend the four hour workshop led by the author. My mindset was that the worst case scenario would be I'd have fun, go on a brave adventure, have a story to tell, and meet a best-selling author. I had nothing to lose.

At the workshop the author taught us to make a vision board. We looked through magazines and found things that aligned with what we wanted out of life. I remember secretly looking for the words "write a book" but not finding them. I don't really remember what else I thought I wanted, but I wish I did. Well, the things I cut from the magazines never made it onto that posterboard. I struggled to decide what belonged on the board and what didn't. I truly didn't know what I wanted anymore.

There were no pictures of my husband in the magazines and what I desperately wanted was him and my old life back. While at the workshop, I briefly met the author. She shook my hand and said, "I don't know if you like to write, but I see writing in your future."

She did not know I had been searching for those words, but her intuition planted the idea that I needed to write a book even deeper within me, even though I didn't know what I thought I would write a book about. I just knew I wanted to write. I went home happy about the trip. All of those things that I mentioned before were great—fun, adventure, meeting the author—but I felt unsettled and worried that I was lost and didn't know where I was going, and I felt very alone and uncertain of myself and my future.

I put finishing that vision board on my to-do list, but somehow I could not envision the poster. I couldn't organize it my mind, perhaps because I wasn't looking for "a man" (didn't want one after Wes) or "a new job" (I had a great one) or "my dream home" (I already had that), but I was trying to manifest a whole new me. A whole new life. I had a proverbial blank canvas in front of me. Staring at a blank canvas can be really exciting and limitless...or completely overwhelming. I felt overwhelmed. I was sure I wouldn't give up though. I have never been a quitter. I have always tried to face my fears and tried to conquer them. When I taught school I had a sign made out of vinyl letters in my classroom that read, "Never give up!" to encourage kids to persevere when things get hard. I could see that sign in my head and I had to listen to my own advice. *Kids can power through hard things, I can too!*

I started going to healing events that I found online. I say "I found," but in truth I believe they were placed in my path. I was not looking for those types of things, but I was hungry for healing and I was open to anything. I knew it would be really easy to fall into destructive habits or into a deeper hole of despair if I didn't do something to keep my head above water.

It seemed everywhere I turned, the Universe was showing me clues, breadcrumbs toward my new path, possibilities for how to heal. As social media goes, you merely think inside your head about getting a new toilet and before you know it your feed is full of all things bathroom-related. I was thinking "HELP!" and the Universe sent a few lifesavers into my Instagram feed. I was open to them and chose to give them a try. One good thing about being at the bottom of a pit of despair is that taking risks doesn't feel like much of a risk when you feel you have nothing left to lose. I found that I really enjoyed those online healing events and met some truly amazing teachers and friends. The events were held online because after I returned home from New York, COVID hit and there were limitations on going out. While COVID was a huge deal and life-altering in so many ways, for me personally at that time, it was a very secondary problem. I was in the dark night of the soul trying to find ways to simply survive my own life.

One of the coolest recurring healing events was an evening of yoga, Reiki, and a brief message from Spirit. Those events were so very healing for the whole me: mind, body, and spirit. One incredible message I received from my husband in Heaven was this: "Tell me what you want in life. Give me your wishes like magic beans and I will help grow them into a beanstalk for you."

Those powerful words inspired me and gave me clarity, not about what I wanted, but about how to go about figuring it out. I also felt it was permission from him for me to be happy, to pursue things that could bring me peace. I was in desperate need of peace.

I purchased a blank sketchbook to get started—not imagining I would ever fill up its 210 pages. I organized the book into categories for all of the different aspects of my life: self-love, home, family, work, spirituality, health, etc. I put those things on tabs and began gluing the magazine clippings from the workshop into the book in the places it felt like they "belonged" and set about figuring out what I wanted. Over time that process felt like it was working. At least it was working to fill my blank canvas and awaken my soul. It took me to a wonderfully hopeful place in my heart and mind each time I worked on it. The sketchbook became my dream book, my vision book, my *Beanstalk Book.*

In the vision board workshop I learned to look through a magazine and if something "resonated" with me then I needed to tear it out. I began doing that like it was my job...because it kind of was...and over the next several months my book was filled.

My heart was healing and my life was changing. Sometimes I go back through and look at how many things in my book have come true. Some were feelings, healings, or attitudes, and some were tangible, physical things, but so many have become reality.

Wes gave me several beautiful messages over the months and he helped me open my heart to many things, including the possibility of love. Because of his healing messages I was able to open my very closed heart to actually loving again, something I never dreamed possible. I was *never* going to love another man. I was planning on a life of being alone forever. I was satisfied with being alone and rediscovering myself and didn't need someone else. What's that saying? Never say never. Yeah, I guess I am learning that.

Incredibly, I am now married to a wonderful soul. His name is Layton and we met through mutual friends about five months before Wes passed away. He and Wes had begun a friendship and when Wes was sick Layton traveled across the state to the hospital several times to visit and pray with Wes. Layton was not only a professional musician, but also a minister, so when Wes passed away our friends took the initiative to ask him to perform Wes' celebration of life. I was not really thinking about what was needed for a funeral. I had never in my 49 years of life ever thought about planning a funeral. I didn't want a funeral and really found it strange to be planning and hosting what was essentially a party during the worst time of my life. What I really wanted was for things to go back to normal.

Layton came and did a beautiful job of singing his amazing songs and encouraging everyone with his inspiring words during the celebration of Wes' life. He took care of many of the details for me and helped to make it a beautiful, touching, and memorable event. It was such a wonderful gift. After the funeral he continued to pray for our family from a distance. He had also lost his spouse to cancer. He understood what I was going through. He and his wife were married for 38 years and had five children together. Interestingly, Layton's wife and Wes had birthdays on the very same day.

Well, a little more than a year into my grieving Layton and I went for coffee together. I thought it would be great to talk to him because of our similar journeys. Turns out I was right. We had the most incredible conversation about life and loss. We talked about dreams shattered and hopes for the future. I told him that I talked to mediums, had life-sized fathead cutouts of Wes at my house, and did all kinds of crazy things in grief. I think I was trying to keep him at a distance and make sure he could see all of my crazy so he would have no interest in me. He was so kind and gentle and didn't judge any of my choices—not out loud anyway! We both expressed our desire to never get married again and he had committed to never having another dog, as he had recently tragically lost his.

How, through all of this talk of loss and heartache, is this coffee conversation so full of laughter and joy? I wondered. After our coffee, we then began talking on a regular basis, and sometimes for hours and hours on the phone, and found that we had so many commonalities, despite the very different lives we had led. We quite quickly and unexpectedly fell in love and a year later got married, and now Layton has another dog. Like I said, never say never!

Layton and I now spend our lives finding joy in each day and healing together. Our beloved spouses in Heaven are a regular and beautiful part of our conversations, our daily lives, who we are, and how we live. We both understand that our spouses in Heaven are and always will be a part of our lives. They were instrumental in making us who we are today. They have shaped us into the person each of us fell in love with. Our grief has united us. Our love is healing us. We have created a safe space in our relationship to talk about and grieve our lost loves as well as rejoice in and nurture our new love. We both understand that it is possible to be heartbroken but also laughing and joyful at the very same time.

I will continue to expand on Layton's and my story throughout the book. So many of the things in my dream book have come as a direct result of our relationship, unrelated to love or companionship even.

I pasted the words "always tidy" and "a put together home" in my vision book. My home had become disheveled and chaotic from life being hectic and especially so in my months of depression and aloneness. I had the desire to get everything back into order and I have always been a bit of a pile person. I normally have a stack of things to be filed, put away, or sorted somewhere in the house and I wanted to change that in myself and have a totally clutter-free space. I joke (or perhaps I am serious) when I say Wes, my husband in Heaven, knew it would be easier to send someone to me who would take care of those things rather than getting my chaotic style of managing things to change. My new love is a terrific life companion who loves incredibly deeply and is a total neat-nick who likes to make sure the house is always tidy and put together nicely. I also put the words "house music" in my vision book. I honestly didn't know what that even meant at the time. I suppose it sounded lovely or something about it spoke to me. Now I know it means the sounds of guitar music in the background as I work from home and my husband, a singer-songwriter, practices his songs in another room.

I also put the words "quit hitting snooze" in my vision book. My whole life I have been so terrible with the alarm clock, hitting snooze until I run out of snoozes. I am not sure how Wes put up with it, quite frankly. Well, since Layton came into my life, I no longer own an alarm clock. I no longer set an alarm to wake up...ever. He is an early riser and he started calling me on the phone with a gentle "Good morning" every day at the time I needed to get up. Now that we are married he continues to get me up on time everyday. I cannot tell you how wonderful it is to be awakened with a gentle nudge, a sweet smile, and a cup of coffee in bed instead of the loud and obnoxious BEEP BEEP BEEP startling me into my days.

So much has changed in my life since I began actively dreaming of and creating my future. The process was this and only this: Put things in the book that resonate. If I liked the look, the feel, the sound, the idea of it—whether it seemed possible or not, whether it seemed reasonable or not, or even whether or not I understood why it appealed to me—I put it in. It was not my job to understand (yet) or to be bothered by how to make it happen. The more we think, the more we judge and let our inner critics have their say. They speak of impossibilities and the shouldn'ts and the don'ts.

I find the process of making my vision book, that I call *Beanstalking,* to be a heart activity and not a head activity. If I allow myself to just go with the flow and lightheartedly "be" while doing this, I find so much joy and I don't worry or fuss about what I am putting in, why I am putting it in. It no longer matters where in the book it goes. The idea is to focus my thoughts, energy, and heart on what I desire. Period.

At first my mom didn't "get" what I was doing. She didn't like that I killed magazines instead of reading them. Magazines have so much more value to me than the stories or pictures. They represent to me limitless possibilities for my own life. Not a written piece of material now gets through my hands without the scrutiny of my eyes scanning it, wondering if there are any great words on it before recycling or throwing it away. It takes so much willpower to not rip things out of magazines at the doctor or dentist's office while I wait to be seen. Even political campaign flyers get my eyes on them - not for the empty promises, but for the " I'll Be The Change"—*Oooh, I like that for me!"*

The tattered spine and cover of my Beanstalk Book.

The well-worn tabs of my Beanstalk Book.

My daughters are seeing how this process has changed my life in positive ways and are beginning their own Beanstalk Books. We have started a Beanstalk Retreat to have time together and to heal and to make their beans grow into beanstalks too. I now have a handful of friends Beanstalking as well.

A soul-sister of mine has found tremendous healing and life changes from this process and we have so much fun visiting while Beanstalking together. She and I both lost our husbands and hated Friday nights after becoming widows because we both had always spent Friday nights with our hubbys. In the past we had looked forward to the end of the week, but after we lost our husbands, Friday night became a source of sadness. We changed that by getting together and cutting and pasting our hopes and dreams while chatting and helping to heal one another's hearts.

Here are a couple of interesting notes about that soul-sister friend. First, we met at a grief support meeting that we both had resisted attending. We went to coffee and cried and talked about our husbands and agreed they seemed to have similar character, interests, and hearts and would have liked each other. Immediately after leaving the coffee shop that day I saw the number 22 along with her husband's unusual first name on the back of a city bus. It really struck me as odd. I then ran into Wes' friend and told him about the weird "coincidence" and he told me he knew my new friend's husband and so had Wes. She and I had just met, but our husbands actually knew each other in life.

The second interesting bit is that Wes had given me a message that I needed to "find joy." I knew that was true as mine had escaped me since his passing, but his message may have had a double meaning. When I went to pick up my new friend to go shopping, her house number had a 22 in it and the street name was Joy! I like to think our husbands had something to do with making sure we met.

I am always finding words and pictures to put in my book. I tear out or cut them and put them in my pile to paste in later. There are times when I go through my "pile" to paste them in and things I cut out have already happened! I saw a great creative storage cart in a magazine. It was a unique way to store multiple ongoing projects in an art work space so I clipped it out, thinking maybe I could recreate it somehow on my own. I placed it in the pile to be glued and forgot about it. When I went to put it in the book I realized that I had actually already found one at a store, identical to the one I had clipped…at 75% off and I snatched it up—before it even made it into the book!

Sometimes I don't remember why I cut something out or what it was about an image that spoke to me. Sometimes I see something I didn't realize I cut out, like the words "having a mentor is always important." I didn't know that I thought that was a thing. I wasn't looking for a mentor, but God put one in my path and I have now been working with a magical mentor for six months and making so many dreams come true. One of them is this book.

As a teacher for 20 years, I have often printed the following poem and given it to my young students. One kindergartner told me her "dad liked it so much he put wood around it". I kept this poem in my heart as I dreamt of the unknowns in my future and I give it now to you as you dare to dream of what could be in yours…

"Listen to the mustn'ts, child. Listen to the don'ts. Listen to the shouldn'ts, the impossibles, the won'ts. Listen to the never haves, then listen close to me… Anything can happen, child. Anything can be."
— *Shel Silverstein*

In the following pages I will guide you as you create a life that makes your desires real and brings you joy. I call this process *The Beanstalk Book: A Magical Guide to Realistically Living Your Enchanted Life.*

Thank you for being with me on this incredibly exciting and fulfilling magical journey.

CHAPTER **TWO**:
INVITATION

I am excited to share with you my vision board in a book! I will walk you through the entire process, answer your questions, encourage you, and lead you on the path to your best life.

To get started you will need a few things. Wait! Don't go get your scissors and glue just yet. You will need some mental preparation and the proper mindset before you cut and paste anything. In making a Beanstalk Book—aka Beanstalking you need to do or have the following:

Willingness to believe that great things can happen for you.

Intuition to allow yourself to open and follow your heart (and your gut) and listen to and trust your inner knowings.

Release and let go of fears and/or face them, understand them, and release them to free yourself to allow joy in.

Hope for the future. Believe in yourself and your potential, your worthiness, and in the magic of the miraculous Universe.

An **open mind and heart.** You will need to shift your awareness from the fixed reality of now to the potential reality of tomorrow.

You may be wondering how does it even work, exactly? Well, the answer is I do not actually know, but I know that it does. I have studied biology and anatomy and physiology so I understand that the systems all have jobs and do them efficiently. But how each system knows how to do their jobs, that I do not know. I do not claim to understand the science or reasoning behind many truths in my life. I do not know how I am able to feel emotions and know love. I just know that I can. I do not understand how my internal organs keep my body temperature regulated and all of my systems functioning, but I know that they do. I have read about quantum physics and I understand the concepts of the quantum field and the Law of Attraction, but I still don't know how it knows how to do what it does. It is the same with this process. I just know that I put things in my dream book and they become real, tangible, measurable, observable things. I just know. This will work for you too.

When I began this process I was not trying to make things happen outside of myself. I was simply trying to feel good on the inside and find enough inspiration to get through the day. Each day, if I could just muster enough strength and fortitude to face and cope with today, then tomorrow I would muster up tomorrow's courage. I was living in the present moment, not by decided intention, but out of sheer survival. If I could keep on mustering strength each day, for that day, then I could keep myself going, keep from giving up, and eventually keep learning and growing enough to stand and feel strong.

At some point I began to bank some of the strength because I was still putting in the same effort, but it didn't take as much energy to stay afloat as I became stronger. Then, on the days that the waves of grief would come up, crash on me, and knock me over, I could rest in my reserves of strength, knowing that I could make it through. All you need to know for sure is that you can do this moment, this hour, this day. Each one going forward will take care of itself as it arrives. In short, work on the now and don't worry about tomorrow until it is the now.

Where to Begin

Let's get started on the process. The first step is to begin taking a look at your life and how you feel. The way to do this is to list all of the areas of your life that are important. I have made a sample list you may use, or make up your own. Then rate each area of your life on how satisfied you are with it. The higher the number the more satisfied. The lower the number the less satisfied.

Notice I don't ask how perfect your life is. This is not about how perfect things are; this is about how you feel about your life and circumstances. The purpose is not to judge, feel shame or overwhelm, but to take control and make things great or see how great they already are. You will have a visual of what you love and don't love about your life right now.

Here's an example of a rating:

I have a satisfaction level of 5 for my home right now, however, someday I would like to put two sweet tiny cabins on the land for visitor guest cabins--but they are not there yet. Still I am satisfied with my home. There is little to no closet space—and I am not exaggerating. There is not a single hanging bar for clothes in my home, but I am still satisfied. How could I be? Why am I satisfied? This home was meant to be a vacation home, so I am living in a vacation home every day of my life. Do you see the beauty in that? I am creative and have learned to live without my walk-in closets. I love my home. Can I improve on it and make it better? Yes, but life would be boring if it were perfect. For me: satisfaction 5. If I died today I wouldn't have any regrets about my home.

On the other hand, a rating of 1 does not mean failure. This is not us being graded on performance. It is how you feel about it.

One reader shared with me her satisfaction with her body/self was a 1. She is healthy, gorgeous, thin, has a beautiful smile, and lights up a room when she walks in—but she feels unsatisfied with her body. There is no shame in that.

We need not judge our own satisfaction levels—perhaps just see where they are and adjust our lives and minds accordingly. This example about body satisfaction simply shows where the focus can be put to best use. Her beauty is already in place; she just needs a shift in her mindset about herself and to see what others see in her.

Most people have a combination of both high and low numbers. Don't judge your satisfaction, just observe it. Below is an example inventory for you to use. Add others or skip areas that do not apply to you.

Home

1	2	3	4	5

Work/Career

| 1 | 2 | 3 | 4 | 5 |

Spirituality

| 1 | 2 | 3 | 4 | 5 |

Romance

| 1 | 2 | 3 | 4 | 5 |

Creativity

| 1 | 2 | 3 | 4 | 5 |

Family

| 1 | 2 | 3 | 4 | 5 |

Adventure

| 1 | 2 | 3 | 4 | 5 |

Self-Care (Feelings/Well-being)

| 1 | 2 | 3 | 4 | 5 |

Friend Relationships (Social Life)

| 1 | 2 | 3 | 4 | 5 |

Physical Self (Diet/Exercise)

| 1 | 2 | 3 | 4 | 5 |

Finances

| 1 | 2 | 3 | 4 | 5 |

Following Dreams (Being True to Yourself)

| 1 | 2 | 3 | 4 | 5 |

Now take a look at the areas you are fully satisfied with. Take a long pause for a moment and really feel it. Feel the joy and gratitude for those areas of your life that are wonderful and bask in the glory of the fulfillment. This is magical.

Now take a look at those areas you would like to work on. If you have no areas of full satisfaction, do not be dismayed. No matter how dissatisfied you are there is always a way to make things better. Be grateful, instead, for the opportunity to change what you do not like, and for this guidebook, right in your hands, that can help you get there.

You now have a quick visual of what you would like to work on. The question you ask now is what makes you happy or unhappy within each area.

The following pages contain is a list of questions to contemplate:

Write your answers to any/all that apply. If this is overwhelming, just pick the area that is the lowest satisfaction level or the area you feel most motivated to change. If even that is overwhelming, pick the area that you feel most confident about changing, even if the changes are small, it is a place to start. This questionnaire does not all have to be done at once. This can take several sittings and can be revisited anytime you like. If there is one thing we know about life it's that it is always changing.

A note for stay-at-home parents: you may use the career section as you choose pertaining to your job within the home/family, or something you wish for in the future when the kids are grown, or skip it and use the home/family sections for your thoughts. You are important, included, and in my heart as I write this. I stayed home with my young children and then I taught for 20 years. I understand both worlds.

Questions to consider about your HOME:

- What do you currently love about your home?

  _____

  _____

  _____

  _____

- What would you change about your current home?

  _____

  _____

_____

_____

- What do you want your home to look and feel like?

_____

_____

_____

_____

- Where would you like your dream home to be? Is your current home where you would like to be or do you wish to move?

_____

_____

_____

_____

- If your current home is your dream home, is there anything that needs to change about it? If you wish to move, describe the details you'd like to see.

_____

_____

_____

_____

- What do you think needs to happen to get you on the path to your dream home?

_____

_____

_____

_____

- Finish the sentence based on your home: *If I knew I couldn't fail and/or weren't afraid, I would*

_____

_____

_____

_____

Questions to consider about your WORK/CAREER:

• What do you currently love about your work?

_____

_____

_____

_____

• What would you change about your current career?

_____

_____

_____

_____

- What do you want your career to look and feel like?

_____

_____

_____

_____

- Describe your dream job.

_____

_____

_____

_____

- What do you think needs to happen to get you on the path to your dream job?

_____

_____

_____

_____

- Finish the sentence based on your work/ career: *If I knew I couldn't fail and/or weren't afraid, I would*

_____

_____

_____

_____

spirituality

**Questions to consider about your
SPIRITUALITY:**

- What do you currently love about your spiritual life?

- What would you change about your current spiritual life?

_____

_____

_____

_____

- What is your spiritual goal?

_____

_____

_____

_____

- List some people, places, events, or ideas you could seek out for more information about having a more spiritually fulfilling life. (if you have no ideas, it's ok; they will come eventually)

_____

_____

_____

_____

- What do you think needs to happen to get you on the path to your spiritual fulfillment?

_____

_____

_____

_____

- Finish the sentence based on your spirituality: *If I knew I couldn't fail and/or weren't afraid I would*

_____

_____

_____

_____

Questions to consider about your ROMANCE:

Note that *romance* does not equal *sex*. Romance is whatever you feel is romantic in a relationship.

- What do you currently love about your romantic life?

_____

_____

_____

_____

- What would you change about your current romantic life?

  _____

  _____

  _____

  _____

- What can you do to be happier with your current romantic situation?

  _____

  _____

  _____

  _____

- Are you currently in a relationship that could use more romance?

  _____

  _____

  _____

  _____

- Are you currently looking for or dreaming of a partner, but do not have one?

  _____

  _____

  _____

  _____

- Describe your ideal romantic relationship.

  _____

  _____

_____

_____

- Finish the sentence based on your romantic life:
  If I knew I couldn't fail and/or weren't afraid I would

_____

_____

_____

_____

creativity.

Questions to consider about your CREATIVITY:

• What do you currently love about your creative expression?

_____

_____

_____

_____

• What would you change about your current creativity?

_____

_____

_____

_____

- What do you want to create?

_____

_____

_____

_____

- Why are you not creating?

_____

_____

_____

_____

- What is stopping you?

_____

_____

_____

_____

- Do you lack the time, the money or the confidence?

_____

_____

_____

_____

- Are you caught up in the outcome or end product?

_____

_____

_____

_____

• Are you afraid of judgment or what someone will think of you or your work?

_____

_____

_____

_____

• Are you blocked creatively?

_____

_____

_____

_____

• What needs to happen to get you on the path to creating?

_____

_____

_____

_____

• Finish the sentence based on your creativity: *If I knew I couldn't fail and/or weren't afraid, I would*

_____

_____

_____

_____

Questions to consider about your FAMILY:

Note that family is as defined by you.

* What do you currently love about your family life?

_____

_____

_____

_____

- What would you change about your current family situation?

_____

_____

_____

_____

- Is there anything within your control to change in your family life?

_____

_____

_____

_____

- Describe how you would like to see your family life change.

_____

_____

_____

_____

- What do you think needs to happen to get you on the path to harmony in your family?

_____

_____

_____

_____

- Finish the sentence based on your family life: *If I couldn't fail and/or weren't afraid I would*

_____

_____

_____

_____

Questions to consider about your ADVENTURE:

Note that *adventure* does not equal *travel*. Adventure is whatever *you* would like it to be.

- What is an adventure to you?

_____

_____

_____

_____

- What do you currently love about your adventures?

_____

_____

_____

_____

- What would you change about this area of your life?

_____

_____

_____

_____

- Are there places you want to go, things you want to experience, or sights you want to see?

_____

_____

_____

_____

- If yes, name three of these things.

_____

_____

_____

_____

- What is holding you back from doing those things? Time, money, fear, no one to share the experience with, other?

  _____

  _____

  _____

  _____

- What do you think needs to happen to get you on the path to more adventure for you?

  _____

  _____

  _____

  _____

- Finish the sentence based on your adventures: *If I knew I couldn't fail and/or weren't afraid I would*

  _____

  _____

  _____

  _____

Questions to consider about your SELF-CARE (feelings/well-being):

- What do you currently love about your emotional well-being?

_____

_____

_____

_____

- What would you change about your current state of well-being?

  _____

  _____

  _____

  _____

- What is the overall state of your feelings?

  _____

  _____

  _____

  _____

- If you had to say, *Most of the time I feel*_____, what would you put in the blank?

  _____

  _____

  _____

  _____

- Do you have a self-care routine that goes deeper than facials, massages, hair or nail treatments, or other material treats or rewards?

  _____

  _____

  _____

  _____

- How do you usually handle your difficult emotions? Stuff them? Cry it out? Yell? Journal? Meditate? Other?

  _____

  _____

  _____

  _____

- What do you think needs to happen to get you on the path to your happiest self?

  _____

  _____

  _____

  _____

- Finish the sentence based on your self and your emotional well-being: *If I knew I couldn't fail and/or weren't afraid I would*

  _____

  _____

  _____

  _____

Questions to consider about your FRIEND RELATIONSHIPS (social life):

- What do you currently love about your social life?

  _____
  _____
  _____
  _____

- What would you change about your current social life?

  _____
  _____

_____

_____

- Do you need more friends, better choice of friends, deeper relationships with current friends, more time with friends, friends with more common lifestyles and time to spend together?

_____

_____

_____

_____

- What can you do to be a friend to others?

_____

_____

_____

_____

- What do you think needs to happen to get you on the path to more fulfilling friendships?

_____

_____

_____

_____

- Finish the sentence based on your friend relationships: *If I knew I couldn't fail and/or weren't afraid I would*

_____

_____

_____

_____

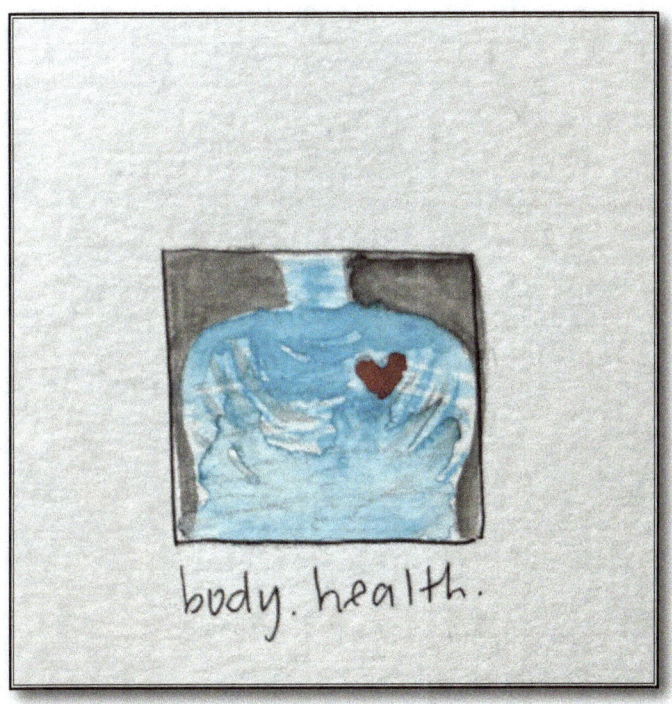

body. health.

Questions to consider about your PHYSICAL SELF (diet/exercise):

- What do you currently love about your body?

_____

_____

_____

_____

- What would you change about your current body?

_____

_____

_____

_____

- Are you struggling with your heath?

_____

_____

_____

- Are you struggling with your body image?

_____

_____

_____

- Are you struggling with your weight?

_____

_____

_____

- How would you like your body to look and feel?

_____

_____

_____

- Are you currently doing anything to be happier with your physical self?

_____

_____

_____

_____

- What do you think needs to happen to get you on the path to loving your body as it is so you can give it what it needs to be at its best?

_____

_____

_____

_____

- Finish the sentence based on your body: *If I knew I couldn't fail and/or weren't afraid I would*

_____

_____

_____

_____

finances.

Questions to consider about your FINANCES:

- What do you currently love or what are you grateful for about your finances?

_____
_____
_____
_____

- What would you change about your current finances? (Silly question, right? *I don't have enough money!*).

_____

_____

_____

_____

- Do you have debt, are you unemployed, or do you not make enough to make ends meet?

_____

_____

_____

_____

- Are you wanting to save, but cannot?

_____

_____

_____

_____

- Do you need a retirement fund or college fund?

_____

_____

_____

_____

- What specifically are you hoping for (besides just *lots of cash*, of course)?

_____

_____

_____

_____

- How much money would you like to earn?

_____

_____

_____

_____

- How much do you dare to dream of making?

_____

_____

_____

_____

- What do you think needs to happen to get you on the path to financial happiness?

_____

_____

_____

_____

- Finish the sentence based on your finances: *If I knew I couldn't fail and/or weren't afraid I would*

_____

_____

_____

_____

dreams

Questions to consider about FOLLOWING DREAMS (being true to yourself):

- What do you currently love about your ability to follow your dreams and be true to yourself?

_____

_____

_____

_____

- What would you change about how you are being true to yourself and your dreams?

  _____
  _____
  _____
  _____

- Finish the sentence (don't judge the answer; just let it be): *My heart wants to*

  _____
  _____
  _____
  _____

- What do you dream of doing? To what extent are you doing that?

  _____
  _____
  _____
  _____

- What activity makes you lose track of time and space? How often do you do that?

  _____
  _____
  _____
  _____

- How would you feel if you could do that as a job?

  _____
  _____

_____

_____

- Describe your ideal day.

_____

_____

_____

_____

- What do you think needs to happen to get you on the path to following your dreams?

_____

_____

_____

_____

- Finish the sentence based on following your heart and dream as your true self: _If I knew I couldn't fail and/or weren't afraid I would_

_____

_____

_____

_____

Now that you've taken inventory and have some ideas of what you are happy with and what you would like to work on, we can move on to how to begin to focus your energies on getting those things.

It can be scary to look at what you wrote. It may make you feel overwhelmed or want to shut down. Perhaps you don't believe you are in control of any of that. Perhaps you don't believe in magic because life is just too real. Perhaps you are energized and excited to see that you do know what you want and you feel the joy of what it will be like to get it. Either way, you are ok. It will be ok. I am here to walk you through this.

We are now going to do another activity.

Go find a magazine. Run and grab anything you have lying around—a catalog, newsletter, any kind of magazine or printed material you can find, even if it doesn't belong to you (we won't be "killing" it right now). This is just an exercise. If no printed materials are available open the Pinterest app or another lifestyle browsing or idea-outlet site on your phone or computer. (I'll wait while you go get it. Sweet instrumental classical music plays in my head. I am patient.)

When I was a kid I used to take a Christmas catalog and a marker or pen and pretend that I was allowed to have one thing on each and every page. I never looked at the prices, sizes, or anything practical. I never thought about where I would put it or how it would fit into my room or even why I would want it—I just dreamed. I circled what appealed to me. I never actually got any of it. That was just childhood dreaming. I never told anyone I wanted any of it. We didn't have a lot of money, so I didn't ever imagine getting any of it—it was just for my own enjoyment. I found that on some pages nothing appealed to me, while other pages had so many great choices I had a hard time deciding what to circle.

This activity we're doing is much the same as that. This is a playful time to just look and see what your heart wants and doesn't want. You may have things in mind that you already know you want, but it's fun to allow your heart to play for a little while. Ok. Now that you have a magazine or some digital media, look through it and let yourself enjoy what you are being drawn to. Do not cut or rip anything out right now—just look and feel. Notice, but do not do anything. Notice when your heart is drawn to something and your mind pipes in with things like *You don't need that? You already have a perfectly fine_____*, or *Having this means giving up that.* Notice these thoughts as they creep in, but keep listening to your heart.

Your *heart* speaks quietly and more peacefully. Your *thoughts* might be louder and perhaps more negative, unsettling, or even demanding. Notice each of them.

When you have finished looking and observing and listening to your body, you may set the magazine aside. If you found something in it that you really are drawn to, you may mark the page, pin it in the app, or rip it out for future use (if the magazine belongs to you, of course).

This activity was not for beginning to cut out anything or starting your book yet. It was about practicing what it feels like to wish, dream, allow, and perhaps hear your own inner critical voices. They may sound like the voices of reason (*You don't have the money, That dream is too big, What would people think?*) but they are your limiting thoughts and beliefs. This activity was for you to simply observe what was happening in you in the moment.

In this beginning exercise you may have had things come up for you—fear, worry, anxiety, or total childlike excitement. All are normal responses. What is normal anyway? That is a whole book by itself! However you responded was the correct response. Whether the things that came up for you were uncomfortable or exciting, we will look into that later. The idea here was to practice noticing and observing.

The beginning stage of this process is when perfectionism practices may begin to show up. I am here to tell you that this book is not a scrapbook, although the physical activity is similar. Here we are not preserving the treasured photos of the past, we are not reminiscing, and we are not creating a visually pleasing masterpiece with a thousand stories told for future generations to enjoy. This is a book for potentially no one to see but you. That is completely up to you. The point of this is not for your book to be seen and enjoyed by others, but to be a personal and continuous work in progress, an ever-changing book of wishes, desires, growth, and proof that you are living and dreaming. It can be messy and incomplete and ongoing. That is the nature of life, and this book reflects life. There may even be things you want for a minute and then you evolve past them. That's ok. They can remain in there even if you no longer want them. They remain as visual stepping stones for getting you closer to your deeper desires.

An example of this is at one time I was looking for front doors that were beautiful and that I wanted to use at my house. For years my husband Wes and I talked about getting a new front door for our home that was built in the late sixties. The door on it was funky, ornate, carved, painted wood. It was a solid door, but we wanted to freshen up the look of the front of the house. So when I started my dreaming after his passing, I looked and looked for images of great front doors and pasted them into my Beanstalk Book.

Later I began to dream of moving to the mountains. The mountain dream came true, but the door dream did not. My daughter and her family now live in our old home. They are fine with the old door, and because I still own the house, perhaps one day I'll give it a new door. My point, though, is that it's ok that my book has doors in it. It doesn't hurt a thing. It reflects where I was at the moment and then my growth beyond those original four walls.

No one needs to see your book so no one will judge your book or your desires. From personal experience, though, if people do see your book they likely won't be judging, they will be in awe and inspired to do the same.

I said that no one will judge your book, which means that you need to be, as the maker and sole viewer, careful not to judge your own work.

Your book can look like a work of art, but it need not be. It is a work of *heart*. That's what is important.

I took an art class in college my freshman or sophomore year and we did a project using collage. I remember the professor sort of shaking his head at my work and saying, "You don't seem to get it." Perhaps he was right, but I am doing this collage for a very specific purpose. My work isn't for someone else, or even for myself, to judge.

It may help in the process if you have a photo of yourself as a child nearby as you work. Ask yourself what you want out of life and treat the answer the way you would treat that sweet youngster. Give yourself the same kind and gentle care you would afford a child. That child is still alive in you, deserving of love and kindness and kind responses to your innermost wishes and wants.

Here is the photo I keep of myself in my workspace. She helps to keep me thinking magically about how I can be anything I want to be when I grow up!

Me as a child, perhaps age 4

Thank you so much for accepting my invitation to join the Beanstalk movement. It is sure to be a magical journey of the heart and soul to places you only thought were in fairy tales! With our minds made up that we truly can make amazing things happen, we can now set about doing them. Let's get on with this party, shall we?

CHAPTER **THREE**:
WHAT DO YOU WANT?

To get what you want out of life, you must first know what you want. If you have no idea what you want, that is ok. I was there once too. I now see my desires crystal clear. I know where I want to go and what I want it to look and feel like. I still have no idea *how* things will happen for me, I just know they will.

I have a great imagination, but God thinks up way better and more amazing things than I do, so I don't want to limit what I want or how I get it by being in complete control. If losing my husband taught me anything...well, it taught me everything, but my point is that one big lesson it taught me is that I am not in control. I always knew that, but somehow over all of the years, I would get caught up in trying to control everything.

I tried to tell myself I was in control of everything: my home, our small business, my teaching job, my family's health and well-being, our schedules, my weight, my marriage and relationships, the weather, the price of a loaf of bread…aaahhhh! I was so wrapped up in trying to make everything just-so that I became overwhelmed and was seriously tired of trying to make everything fit within the box of my life. I was not in control of any of it. I had a part to play, but control was not my role. I needed to learn to allow.

I am apparently really thick-headed because it took the loss of my husband to teach me that I, in fact, am not in control. I am the main character in the show that is my life, but what happens around me is not for me to be in charge of. I can choose where to live and where to work and to have the best attitude and do my best in all situations, but I cannot control it all. Going with a theater metaphor, I can control my own actions, the wardrobe, and the set, even ticket prices and advertising, but I cannot control who buys tickets and shows up, who loves or hates the show, who heckles me in the middle of a dramatic scene, or if another character forgets their lines or doesn't show up…or passes away. I can only be in charge of me and where I hope the story leads.

Now let's continue the process of you and your Beanstalking…

Feel

I want you to look back at your inventory. Look at any area that you completed. If you did them all, choose one area or skim through each for this activity.

Look at your answers to the questions to notice any places where you feel the need to control the outcome. This might be difficult to do at first, but give it a try. As you read through the things you want to see happen in the different areas of your life, *feel* them. By this I mean notice what it feels like to have them be already come true.

An example might be that you want to move up in your company at work. You know this is what you want, you know it's possible with your line of work, you know you are worthy and qualified, but when you *feel* it happening, your heart stings a little. Sit right there for a moment. You got all that you wanted…but try to identify the sting. The sting may be that you will make more money than your spouse, outshine a colleague or sibling, or there may be some other part that you want to control, but cannot. *Notice* the feeling. Feel what it feels like to sit in that for a moment, and then, if you can now take a deep breath and release all of the desire to control the things that are not yours to control—someone else's pay scale, status, feelings, desires, when and how things happen, how others react. This takes time, practice, and reflection. Keep working on it as we progress through this process.

We need to begin to understand a few things. First, we need to become clear about our desires. Next we need to let go of control of things beyond our capacity. Last, we need to allow for variances in how and when our dreams come true. The beauty is that they will!

Surrender

I remember one moment of giving up control and allowing that was one of the most powerful moments of my life. I was in the waiting room of the hospital after my husband collapsed at home. He was taken by ambulance to the emergency room and we were sent to the "family waiting room." I knew in my gut that was a bad sign right then. I had been in the ER waiting room many times for different reasons throughout the years and never was I put in the family waiting room.

The room was small and sparsely decorated, but private. I remember several comfy chairs, boxes of tissue on the side tables and one picture on the wall. It was the most beautiful picture of the face of Jesus. I have seen lots of pictures of Him and some just don't seem like the Him I know in my heart. That was *Him*. I saw that picture, stared deep into it. Looking back, I am not sure if I physically dropped to my knees or if it happened inside me spiritually, but I dropped to my knees in complete surrender and I silently said, "Your will be done". I gave up all control at that moment and surrendered, knowing that I could not be the one to help or save my husband.

I have no idea how long we were in that room, but after a time the doctor came to us and said he was gone. There are no words to describe the devastation and the brokenness of my heart. I was, at that moment and for a long time after that, a walking zombie, a shell of a human— living and breathing with what seemed like a chest full of shards and pieces of my broken heart. That sounds like a terrible example of giving up control being a good idea. Me giving over to God's will took my husband and my children's father—why would that be a good thing? Well, it wasn't!

When I got my heart pieces all back into a pile (that still didn't resemble a heart, but at least they were all in one tidy pile, like when you sweep up a broken glass off of the floor and it's not back into the shape of a glass, but you have all of it in the dust pan), I regretted it. I regretted surrendering. I became so very angry at God for taking Wes. I trusted Him to heal Wes, to make him whole and healthy again. I trusted him to return him to me. How could I ever pray again and expect that God would have my best interest at heart? *That* is not what I prayed for. I assumed in my prayer that God's will and my own were the same, that we both wanted Wes to be okay. I thought He loved me. I was devastated.

Well, now that my heart is back to the shape of a heart—all those shards and pieces glued back together so that it looks like a heart—I see things very differently. I don't regret that prayer to turn over control. I know that Wes would have spent the remainder of his life (perhaps 12-18 months) in a hospital bed, fighting cancer, feeling sick, and withering away. No one gave us hope that he would recover. His cancer was terminal and aggressive. But I had so much hope and thought I was going to take control and make it better.

A difficult but beautiful and healing message I received from Wes in spirit was that he chose to go when given the opportunity. He didn't want to spend the rest of his days in the hospital and having his kids watch him become weak and frail. He is now whole and happy and perfect. After receiving that message from him I realized that I got exactly what I prayed for: My husband is whole and healthy and returned to me again. It looks different than I had imagined, but it is better for Wes. It is how he could go with dignity. Wes apologized for leaving us so soon. I am grateful he didn't have to linger, although I would have taken more time with him no matter what that time was like. I am finally at peace with how he left this world and I am no longer mad at God. He sees so much more of the big picture than I do.

My heart is still healing. It looks completely back to a heart shape, but it will always have the cracks where it was glued back together. There are small pieces that cannot be found to fill some of the gaps. It can function as it once did and is a bit more fragile than it once was, but somehow a bit stronger too. It will never be the same though. Ever.

The lesson here is that allowing, in life, will not always look like the result you want. It may not take you on the route you might like, but it will lead to the path that is meant for you and for those on the journey with you. I now have learned to allow and be more patient (I still struggle with patience). When I allow and give up control I see the power of the Universe and God and watch amazing things happen.

Let Go

Here is an example of how I set an intention and then let it go, released it, and allowed things to happen.

I wrote the letter below in October of 2021. I was to get married to Layton in January and we wanted a home in the mountains. My fiancé, and his late wife had always dreamed of retiring to one particular sweet, small mountain town, Red Lodge, Montana. Wes and I dreamed of retiring somewhere in the Beartooth Mountains—the same mountain range that Red Lodge sits in. It only made sense that Layton and I wanted to carry on that dream together, so we dreamed up our ideal home and wrote the following letter.

We wrote the letter and then tucked it away in my Beanstalk Book and forgot about it. We did not forget about the dream, just the letter.

On the day that we were married, January 22, 2022 a house was listed for sale. When I woke up the next morning the real estate app I had been using to search for a home sent me an alert. *Ding! New home listing!* I opened the app and looked at the home. My heart skipped a beat. It looked like the place we had been looking for.

First thing Monday morning we called for an appointment to look at it. We fell in love with it. It is now ours!

Comparing it to the home described in our letter above: It has year-round access, 1500 square feet, an art studio and writing loft for me, a porch with mountain view for Layton to write his music, a guest bedroom, and two acres for adding guest cabins or camping. The kitchen is new and clean, but with all vintage appliances and cabinets, and the floors are red—*talk about a cool vibe!* Oh, and it came fully furnished. These pictures show the similarities of what I dreamed and what we got.

The dream house cut from a magazine compared to the magical home we have now. It's better than the dream.

DREAM BOOK

REALITY

The vibe I dreamed of and the fully furnished house with the same vibe that we got in our magical new home.

Notice that the timing did not fit into "my plan," but, again, the control thing. The timing was perfect. It was listed on our wedding day and the seller was selling because he, too, lost his spouse to cancer and wanted to pass along their second home to someone who would find joy in it, as his time there was over.

When I look at the letter I see where the sting in my heart would be: the timing. I wanted to control the when. I wanted it to happen before we got married, so we could have our wedding there and make the most beautiful first memory at our new home. That timing was impossible. We needed to wait for the previous owner to be ready to let go of his dream cabin that he'd shared with his late wife. If I had known that had to happen for our dream to be realized, I would never have put a timeframe on it.

I have learned to trust the timing. You too can learn to let go and allow.

The first beautiful memory we have of our home is meeting the previous owner while we were there viewing it and we learned of the passing of his wife. He was in the garage at the time so we were able to meet him and share in his pain and feel the energy his wife left in the home. That was a beautiful gift for us. He comes over to visit us now and again, to sit on the porch and breathe in the air, back again in the place where he and his wife dreamed up their perfect home. That is a gift we can give back to him. That turned out to be a blessing all around, and I learned that I can dream up all of the specifics I like, but the timing and the how are not my worries. So many things had to happen and so many lives were intertwined to make the perfect outcome.

Trust

As you begin the next step, take as much time as you can with your inventory. It can be a work in progress. It can change daily, weekly, monthly. Make changes to it as you see fit, to allow for the inner workings of your heart, divine timing, the miraculous inter-workings of God and the magic of the Universe. Your heart is beginning to know what it wants. That is a big step. You do not need to know how to get there. You do not need to know when it will happen. Focus on what you *are* in control of.

The next steps are the ones that are the hardest for me, because I can be impatient, but trusting that your dream will come true and waiting for the right timing is another part of this process. While there are times that things begin changing overnight or things happen very quickly, there are also times when it seems they will never come true. It's normal, and easy, to lose hope if you don't see evidence of change, growth, or forward movement. When this happens it's good to have a plan because giving up is not an option. Changing your mind is always allowed, but giving up on yourself is not!

Tools

Some things I do when I start to feel like the Universe is not going to deliver what I want, that God is not going to answer the prayer for my desires, or that I am feeling stuck or impatient are the following: meditation, reading inspirational stories, seeking out joy and playfulness, spending time in nature, and journaling.

Meditation

I, personally, do best in meditation when I have a voice guiding me (otherwise I get lost in random thoughts and think about something stupid I said to someone yesterday and then sit with the pang of regret and wonder why I am such a fool and then wonder why they want to be friends with me in the first place...Oh, the mind. It can take me down a rabbit hole in no time flat—Or I will think about what I must do tomorrow and begin to make my grocery list. Or...or...or, you know, a million other things) so I use apps (Breethe and Insight Timer) to find meditations that help me stay positive and present in the moment. There are also many free meditations on YouTube. You could look there for something that suits you, if guided meditation works for you, or at least give it a try.

If you are someone who can meditate without guidance, first, I'll say, "Yay, you!" That is amazing! Perhaps meditating through the rough patches will help you as well.

Meditation is such a very effective tool for me to get and stay on track with my goals, thoughts, and emotions. Praying is when we talk to God and meditating is when we listen for answers. When I find myself slipping into not trusting or being impatient, meditation can usually get me back to center.

Distractions

Another method for keeping me on track with believing, trusting, and being patient is good, old-fashioned distractions. I use caution when turning toward social media as a distraction, but I do use it. I follow several very inspirational people who post words of encouragement, poems, art, and amazing and true beautiful human stories, and I find that to be a helpful place to run into the right words or personal connection to keep me on track. I use caution because it can also lead to a rabbit-hole of wasting time and making myself feel worse, or doubting myself altogether because I compare myself to others.

I do not follow news or politics on social media. I am intentional about only ingesting inspirational things online. The more I follow inspirational people and groups, the more the "suggested for you" tips I receive align with what I enjoy. I guess the social media algorithm is a bit like the Universe's—it sends you more of what you are looking for. I never go looking for a debate or discussion in this arena. I search for love, light, inspiration, kindness, connection with people, and joy. A great inspirational book is perhaps a better source, but is not always readily available like social media is.

Play

The best distractions for me are play-related. I love to play! Play makes me feel alive and hopeful and full of joy. I play with my dog, play a card game with my husband, put together a puzzle, or play through creating art. I color, sing, dance, create, talk to others about ridiculous things, read children's books, swing, talk to a child. Finding myself in play helps me to stay happy and focused and the happier I remain, the more hopeful I feel about my visions, dreams, wishes, and prayers.

Playing games online or on my phone does not have the same affect as other playing. It makes me feel guilty for wasting time and lazy for sitting around, maybe because it feels somehow addictive to me—I am not sure. So I, personally, stick to non-digital play when the goal is distracting myself from feeling impatient.

Natural Distractions

Nature is a beautiful distraction...quite literally. I am lucky enough to live in the mountains and have beautiful views and trees and places to hike right outside my door. I also don't have to go far to find a river or stream. I find so much peace in nature. The wind on my face, even when it's bitterly cold, makes me feel alive and hopeful.

Find what makes you feel that way. You may not have mountains and rivers and hiking trails, but all you really need is a patch of grass, a park bench to listen to the birds, a fountain of trickling water, a tall tree to sit under, a pile of earth or sand to put your toes in, a window to feel the warmth of the sun on your face...the smallest bit of nature can have a big impact on your heart and mind.

Nature is the best reminder to be present in the moment and trust and be patient. Nature is always in the present. Trees don't think about the past and regret losing their leaves. Losing their leaves is a part of the plan. The wind doesn't worry and wish it blew the other direction. It just blows. Birds don't think about if they are fat or should lose a few ounces. They just live in the moment and fly and flitter and sing and look for something to feed their bellies. Ants don't run to get where they are going (unless they're being chased, of course. That's the only time I run too!), but they lift the found piece of broken potato chip and slowly and steadily follow the path back to the ant hill, carrying their treasure—a load bigger than themselves. They just go, and get there.

Watching these moments in nature gives me glimpses of how to have patience and trust the timing of my life. I find that when I discover what I want, I also get impatient and want it right now. I sometimes feel like if it doesn't happen now I will run out of time. Nature helps me come back to

Earth and slow down and remember that everything happens when it is supposed to, and if there is nothing within my control to do right now then I must keep a positive attitude and let nature remind me to be patient and trust.

Journaling

I also find journaling helpful to keep me focused and be patient and trust that there are things going on in the Universe that I am not able to see that will make my dreams a reality. When journaling in this stage of the process I like to start with gratitude and then continue the dream on paper or perhaps write a letter of thanks for getting the dream (as though it is already done), or live in the dream as though it is currently happening.

Here's and example: If you want a dream vacation to Hawaii, journal about the trip:

Wow! What a beautiful view from this window in first class! There is so much leg room. I have never been in first class before. This is fun! I see the land and sea coming closer to me as the airplane descends. I can imagine how wonderful it will feel to swim in that beautiful water. I step off the airplane and I am hit with an amazing salty warm breeze that envelops me and feels like a hug on my skin. We pick up our rental car and find out we got a free upgrade and are so thrilled to be breathing the ocean air as we drive in this Mustang convertible. This trip is amazing. After checking into our luxury room with a spectacular balcony overlooking the ocean, we decide to take a walk on the beach. I feel my feet in the soft, warm sand. Ah! It feels heavenly…and that ocean view…I see…

You get what I'm saying, right? Live it!

Be there in Hawaii and enjoy the experience with all of your senses before it even happens. It's like practicing for vacation! Get lost in the beauty and fun of it, not the details of a carefully planned itinerary or overstuffed carry-on bags in the airport. Also be careful that you are not trying to control it and create so many expectations that it has to be perfect. Just lean into the *joy* and *relaxation* as you imagine it.

I read somewhere that worrying about a future event makes you have to experience it twice. You worry about getting a shot at a doctor's office, and then you get the shot. You experienced it twice. This is just like that....only wonderful! You get to practice your vacation and then go on vacation. You get to experience it twice...or three times or as many as you like! I love this!

I find any kind of journaling to be helpful. Sometimes you need to rant and rave about things that are frustrating, complain about your bad day, or process emotions on paper or scribble really hard. Those are all therapeutic for me at times. For this step in the Beanstalking process, when you are feeling stuck or impatient, I recommend turning toward gratitude and imaginative journaling. This will keep you hopeful and not entertaining thoughts of doubt or self-pity.

In the process of discovering and getting what we want, we must remember to dream big and be specific, allow the Universe to work its magic and surprise us, release control, be patient, and trust.

CHAPTER **FOUR**:
YOUR LIFE NOW

For this chapter you will need to start by attending a funeral. Not the funeral of a beloved human or family pet but for a word. The word *can't* must die! When I taught 3rd grade I had the privilege of team-teaching with a dear friend of mine. She had the brilliant idea of having an all-out funeral for the word *can't*, to change the mindsets of our students to *can*. We had the students write the word *can't* on sticky notes and then ceremoniously bid good-bye to it as they threw their written words into the trash (burning would have been a way cooler ritual, but lighting stuff on fire is not really a thing in schools, ya know, so we had to improvise).

I am going to ask you to do the same now, with a bit of an adaptation. First, get a piece of paper and write the words *I can't* at the top. Next, set a timer for two minutes and quickly jot down all of the things you think you can't do. Ready...go!

Now that the list is made, read it and reject it. Destroy it—in any way that feels good to you. Rip it into a hundred pieces, burn it (please take safety precautions if you do this—I don't want to have anyone to get hurt on my watch), crumple it beyond recognition, scribble all over it with black marker or crayon. Destroy it in some other way that feels good to you.

Can't is now dead. You are done with it and it no longer has a place in your vocabulary. (Note: I want to make sure you know I mean this only in the terms of the word *can't* as a limiting belief keeping you from doing things. You can still use it as a means to set healthy boundaries for yourself and your family. Please use it to say things like,"I can't go to that event with you today because I need to have some alone time," or "No, honey, you can't go to that party because I am the mom and I said so." Those uses are fine, and necessary. But you may no longer use the word *can't* to describe your abilities or your dreams or your future.)

You Can

When we did the *can't* activity at school there would usually be discussion and blow-back from the students. We taught them well during math and science lessons about probability and using the words *certain, possible, impossible, probable*. They listened and learned. They would say things like, "It's true to say, 'I can't fly, it's impossible". I would say, "Yes, you can fly. You can get on an airplane or a hang glider and fly." They would come back with, "But not with wings, like on my own." I then would tell them to close their eyes and we would take a journey in our minds. I would explain in detail the feelings and the sights and sounds and we would use our imaginations to fly. After that I would tell them to think of a book in which a character flew on a dragon or flew all on their own, magically.

We can all fly in some way or another in our minds or dreams or meditations or while reading a great book. If we imagine good enough, our minds don't know the difference between real and imagined flight. Truly, we can do anything! That is the mindset you need for this process as well. *Anything* is possible, no matter how improbable it may be. Thank goodness the Wright Brothers had the *can* mindset too!

When you find yourself thinking you *can't*, catch yourself and simply change the thought to *can*. Don't even worry about the how!

Now go back to your inventory again. Look at all of the things you wished you could change about your life. Re-read them with "I *can*" before each one.

Here's an example: In the PHYSICAL SELF section, you may have written "I would like to lose 50 pounds." Say this out loud "I *can* lose 50 pounds."

Do this with as many of your statements on your inventory as possible. I challenge you to rephrase all of it to say, "I *can*," even if it doesn't make a coherent sentence—just think of it as *possible*.

If this triggers you in some way when you say the statements as actual possibilities but inside you don't believe it and it makes you feel worse, then stop. Try, at first, "I am open to believing I *can*." This will be a stepping stone to saying and believing that you truly *can*.

No More Apostrophe T

An example of me having to really work hard to change my mindset is with singing. My whole life I have said emphatically, "I can't sing!" In second grade I had a music teacher. She was a nun. I do not recall her name or what she looked like, only her words and how she made me feel. One day I was singing loudly during class—really belting it out because singing was fun and it made me happy. She stopped the class and singled me out, trying to figure out who was the one singing so horribly loudly. She asked me to come to the front of the room and sing in front of everyone. I was a shy child, but had found my confidence in singing somehow, and did as I was told. She then scooted me back to the risers to join the class. As she did that she whispered in my ear, "You should not sing out loud in front of people anymore." Being an obedient child who had just had her only confidence shattered, I never sang out loud in front of people again. My dogs, my toys, and my houseplants sometimes would hear a song or two, but no human ears heard me sing for 20 years or more.

When I had my children I sang to them, but never with others around. When I was in college I had to learn how to teach music, because some schools don't have music teachers. I thought I would die when I had to sing "If You're Happy And You Know It" in front of my peers. I didn't die and no one even flinched or covered their ears. I assumed they were just being polite.

I finally started singing out loud to my husband, Wes, after enough years of marriage that he would be attached enough not to leave me for my horrible singing. And it wasn't until I began sharing my experience with my students that I really changed my mindset about singing. Telling the students and then singing for them had them exuberantly shouting and clapping and telling me my teacher had been wrong. My husband Layton now tells me the nun was wrong. He's a professional singer/songwriter, so I can take his word for it.

So, I am here to tell you that I can sing. I do sing. I love singing. Music makes me really happy. I will not be auditioning for a reality TV talent contest, but *I can sing*!

If you are a journaler, I suggest exploring things you feel like you can't do in your writing sometime. Perhaps look for the incident, person, or experience that gave you the limiting belief and explore why you feel the way you do. Try changing your mindset about those things by rephrasing the words and reframing your thoughts. Try proving yourself wrong!

Growth

As you do these small exercises and reflect on your desires and your current mindset and limiting beliefs you will begin to see changes. This is a nonlinear change. It isn't like learning to tie your shoes—straightforward and once you get it you are done. This may look more like a slow transformation where you gradually begin to notice your own thoughts and beliefs and inner thought programs. It is very magical when you catch yourself thinking and feeling differently in situations than you once did.

Think of this like seasons. When summer comes to an end it begins with slightly cooler temperatures. Then even cooler temperatures and longer periods of cool. Then there are a few days of hot weather again, until finally summer gives way to fall with all of the changes in full color. As time goes on and the temperature again begins to shift and the days get shorter, fall succumbs to winter. This is a little how mindset shift feels, slow and transformative.

Changes in life can be slow, and change can be fast. I feel like I always want change to be fast, but it isn't always that way. If I really stop to think about that, I am glad that some change is slow, even though it makes me crazy with impatience. Perhaps a lesson that I am meant to learn in this life is patience. The reason I believe that some change has to be slow is that we grow slowly, as humans, and although we think we are ready for something as soon as we dream it up, God truly knows best about when we are ready.

Some examples of God knowing best with divine timing and time delays are: having a baby, buying a house, moving to a new city or country, changing career paths, meeting the love of your life, etc. When we realize we would like to have or do one of these big life changes, we usually have time to wrap our brains around the ideas, budget for them, adjust our lives and schedules for them, prepare mentally for new tasks, new routines, new people. We also need to make space, energetically, for these changes. We need our hearts to be open and ready for all of the newness, new emotions, new situations and growth. We need our minds to be ready to gather new information, to learn and adjust to new ideas and circumstances.

The Gift of Time

The time between what we are being gifted and when it arrives is truly a blessing. It allows for us to ready the nursery before the baby comes, pack the boxes and perhaps get rid of few things before moving; learn about the culture, language, or layout of a new place before relocating; gather new skills, wardrobe, or resources for a new career; or release old hurt, loss, wounds, or expectations from past relationships before finding the right one.

All of these things take time and some happen very gradually. If you ask a pregnant woman nearing her due date, she'll likely not agree, but the wait time between conception and birth is a beautiful gift. The slow growth of the baby gives us time to prepare (as best we can for the unknown), to watch the miracles happen within your body or your partner's body, to share the excitement with grandparents, family, and friends, to shop for baby things, dream up the perfect name, and learn what we can about caring for and feeding a newborn. These in-between times allow us to prepare, but they also give us the joy of anticipation and the excitement of looking forward.

I am a pretty spontaneous person and embrace change, but if I had to go straight from conception to birth with no prep time, let's be honest, I would freak out! Or if I found my dream home and had to move in on the spot I wouldn't be ready. The gift is in the pace. The wait time allows us to appreciate what we have when we finally get it. I remember when my husband Wes and I bought our "forever home," as we called it, the dream house that we could stay in forever and raise our kids in. After nine months of searching for a house we *both* loved, we immediately fell in love with a house, that was out of our budget. We felt so deeply that it was meant for our family that we worked to make it happen. There were negotiations, contingencies, bank snafus, and delays. It seemed like it would never happen, but things eventually fell into place and it did happen. It took several months and I thought the wait would kill me.

That wait time that I hated was a gift that lasted for years. Every time I drove up to my home, from the first day we purchased it and for years afterward, I would say as I pulled in the driveway, "I can't believe I get to live here." Worth every day of waiting!

We lived in that house for more than 20 years. We raised our daughters and dogs and cats, a rabbit, a hedgehog, three cows and several horses while we lived there. It was our dream home. It did its job beautifully and I will always love that place.

After Wes passed away and I remarried, I moved to the mountains and now that house where Wes and I raised our family is enjoyed by my daughter and her family and critters. It was not meant for forever, but for a season.

The slow, transformative change of seasons helps us to enjoy this moment and anticipate, with excitement, the next. Thank goodness the trees keep their leaves long enough to enjoy the color changes before they fall to the ground and are covered with snow. Thank God the rain sticks around long enough in the spring for the flowers to get their fill to grow and bloom. Each of these in-between times is beautiful and should be savored. They are moments unto themselves. They are the journey. They are the moments when you have growing pains and you sweat and bleed and cry. They are the moments that make the destination even sweeter and more satisfying in the end. If everything we ever wanted came to us exactly how and when we wanted it, then, sure, we would have it all, but it would be anticlimactic and rather boring. Think of a child who has everything he ever dreamed of handed right to him. Oftentimes he never feels any sort of satisfaction and is left wanting more, despite having it all.

The magic of the journey toward getting it, the visible clues and signs that show us it's coming, and all of the anticipation are truly much of the joy of getting what we want out of life. When we get instant gratification we tend to think, *That's great. Now what?* There is a greater depth of appreciation for, and more intense enjoyment of, the things we work toward or have to wait for than those that come easily. Don't get me wrong, if the Universe dropped a huge surprise of a dream trip around the world on me, I'd be plenty happy. Surprises are a joy! When things we want come to us easily and quickly it is fun and exciting. However, if you can see the wait time as a gift from the Universe, you can give yourself the gift of enjoying the journey while you wait for the amazing to appear in your life. How empowering it feels to not only appreciate the dream in the end, but to cherish the time it takes to get there.

Enjoy the Journey

A sort of literal example of enjoying the journey is road-tripping. My late husband and my current husband and I all love(d) to travel by car. I also love random roadside attractions. As we travel from point A to point B we get to have all kinds of quality time. We spend hours talking about everything under the sun, listening to audio books together, reading books out loud to each other, or singing as we take in the sights around us and see new and wonderful things. We see quaint little places and roadside attractions that we might have missed if we were flying to get where we're going. Sure, it takes longer, but it makes the journey as fun as the destination. There are times when flying is the best way to get where we are going. There is not a thing wrong with flying, but learning to enjoy the drive is priceless.

Whether your dreams are big or small, whether your life is amazing (but something is missing), whether your life is running amuck, has been ripped out from under you, or any combination of the above, you can use this process of Beanstalking to change your life and turn your dreams into reality.

Relax. Keep believing. Never give up. Allow room for surprises. Great things will come, so enjoy the journey.

CHAPTER **FIVE**:
DESERVING

One of the hardest and most important lessons I learned in my life was learning to love myself. All through my life I struggled with loving who I am. I always compared myself to others and came to the conclusion that the other person, whoever it was, was more than me—more pretty, more funny, more intelligent, more successful, more efficient, more organized, more calm, more patient, more talented, and so on. All of my life I felt less. I never felt worthless, but definitely worth less than others and less worthy of great things. I grew up thinking that saying kind or true things that are positive about yourself was considered bragging, and bragging was most definitely not a good thing. I wanted to be good, so rarely did I even try to *think* of something great about myself. I just tried hard not to fail at everything and worked hard on being good to others and giving all things my best effort.

When Wes came along in my life it was so beautiful. We made a wonderful pair. We loved each other so much and truly had each other's best interests at heart. We had a beautiful relationship. He, over the course of 31 years in my life, made me feel important and smart and worthy of love, worthy of success and happiness. He treated me like a princess, but also like an equal partner. While I was with him, I did not have to come up with something nice about myself because he did it. He brought out the great things in me. All was good. I was valued and flourishing. Then he died.

Eeerrrrrrrch!!!!! (Screeching tire coming to a halt) *Wait, what? Now what do I do?*

I lost my best friend and companion, lover, and life partner. As if that weren't bad enough, I had to come to grips with the fact that the one person in the whole world who knew me and thought I was beautiful, kind, loving, sweet, smart, fun, funny, and worthy was gone! Wes leaving took away my worthiness to be loved because he was *the one* person who thought I was all that! It added, for me, another whole layer of grief, or perhaps just an excuse for self-pity, but the sadness surrounding it was real. I wrongly made it someone else's job to love me, in lieu of loving myself.

My Job

With Wes gone, I realized I had to take up the torch for him. I had to love me as well as he had so that I could be, would be, worthy. I set out on my journey to see the beauty in myself. Being older, wiser, and my "give-a shit-ter" completely broken, I knew I needed to do whatever I could to look at myself and see what he saw, if it were possible. I needed to see something to make my life worth continuing. That sounds so dire, but really it was.

I knew that I was absolutely being no good to the world curled up crying on my chair. If I was going to keep going I needed to get myself back to a place where I had something to offer the world again. I was in therapy at the time and my therapist asked what I did for self-care. I couldn't come up with much—an occasional pedicure, a treat of some kind after I completed a goal, but not much else. Looking back now, I see that even the things I did for self-care were not meaningful, good-for-the-soul types of things. They were usually superficial fixes to make me feel prettier, and they almost always had to be "earned" by finishing a major task, project, or goal. I had never put self-care anywhere on or near the top of the priority list and certainly would not treat myself to those luxuries without feeling like I did something to deserve them.

My therapist helped me to realize that I didn't really know how to "do self-care." Then she asked me a stinger of a question: "Do you think your daughters know how to do self-care?" *Oh my gosh!!! What have I done?* I was so busy giving to the world and loving those around me that I forgot about me and, in doing so, I modeled to my children how to give until there is nothing left. *Yikes!* I knew then that I needed to start really loving myself. I had failed myself and my kids, but had been afforded the time to fix it.

Thus began my quest for self-love.

Through the Beanstalk process, I have come so far and am proud to say that I love and appreciate myself deeply. I see my beauty and I work to take care of myself with meaningful self-care routines, gentle kindness toward myself, and seeing my own worth. I now practice self-care as a priority and don't have to earn it. I know that I inherently deserve it and it is imperative for my well-being and my mental health. It also greatly affects my feelings of satisfaction in all of the other areas in my life. This process can help you come to a more loving agreement with yourself too.

To begin, I looked through magazines for words that I wanted to be true of my thoughts and feelings toward myself—the way I wanted to *feel*. My dream book's first category was SELF LOVE. Here are a few pages of my Beanstalk Book from that section:

Just pasting words in the book is not good enough to manifest a true, deep self-love, but it is a really great start. Knowing how I wanted to feel was the beginning of getting there. I considered that the first step and then continued to go back to it again and again. That gave me the goals of how I wanted to feel and how I wanted to see myself and feel about myself and my new life circumstances.

From there I began to get ideas and motivation and strength to get there. As I grew, I also continued pasting and my goals became bigger and better and my love grew deeper. I considered it a practice. Practice is how we get good at things, how we make them stick. When I was teaching I would tell the kids that and they would say, "Yeah, my coach said, 'Practice makes perfect." I would tell them, "That can only be true if your practice *is* perfect." I prefer the words *practice makes permanent*. What you practice (a bad habit or a good one) becomes your permanent practice.

An example is when I taught cursive to third-graders. Sometimes there would be kids who had already learned to write in second grade. They may have practiced their letters over and over until they had muscle memory on how to make them. The problem was that they learned them, or at least practiced them, incorrectly and had permanently imprinted how to do it wrong, so we had to practice a whole new way to form the letters to make their cursive legible and the letters flow into one another. Practice, in that case, did not make perfect.

I did the same thing when I practiced all of those years of giving until I was spent. Fortunately for us humans, we are malleable, and even a habit I practiced all of my life that had become a permanent part of me actually wasn't permanent and could be practiced away…to a more perfect practice of permanence—one of loving myself.

One day, after many months of practicing a new way to talk to myself, of speaking of my strengths and gifts and worthiness and being grateful for my inner beauty and outer talents, I spontaneously wrote the words, "Thank you, God, for all that I am and all that I have." I had been writing freely, but those words stopped me in my tracks. I broke down in tears of joy. *I did it. I love me! I love all that I am! Oh the joy!* Not that all was perfect after that, but that was a beautiful and clear breakthrough for me.

I know that no matter where you are on the scale of self-love and healthy self-care, you can create a practice that creates a permanent love within you too.

Do Whatever It Takes

At one point in my journey to self-love I had photos taken of myself. I had never done that before. There were always pictures of my children and sometimes family portraits, but never just me. I decided that I needed to do it for myself. I would have pictures I could look at that would make me feel beautiful on the outside at the same time as I was doing work on myself on the inside.

I found a photographer with a tender heart and kind soul who made it feel safe for me to be brave. I was really kind of hoping she would doctor the photos up real nice so I looked perfect. She didn't, and that would have defeated the purpose. They were real. They were me in my happy place. They were taken at the cabin, a place where Wes and I had spent many weekends enjoying each other, our family, friends, and the outdoors.

The whole process of the photo shoot and being at the cabin without Wes and being the center of attention in the photos was really hard for me. It made me feel very vulnerable, but in the end was also really healing. I can now look at the pictures and see a strong and beautiful person on a journey to heal and become whole again. Beyond the physical, for me these photos show my inner strength to keep living. They show a woman with her dog working together to move forward from having lost their person and with a knowing that she needed to stay alive in her life for her kids…to really live life for herself.

I encourage you to do whatever it takes—crazy ideas, simple acts, *whatever it takes* to love who you are. Ask yourself and your heart, what you need and then be brave, take a risk, and do it!

Photo credit: Joanna Moss Photography

Make It a Habit

Practicing listening to your heart and your inner child is a daily job. The more we are in tune with what makes us happy, the more opportunities we have to do those things and the more we do them, the happier we are.

In the list below are some ideas that work for me. Please take what you can from me, but discover your own things. What makes your heart sing? It can truly be anything. Doing *that* is how you truly show love to yourself.

I have a glass board hanging in my home that has a to-do list written in wet-erase marker, so it can be easily changed. I use dry-erase marker to fill in the boxes every day or every few days as I mark off things and start again. I need to repeat these things often to keep myself feeling good and connected to my own heart and joy.

These are some things that make me calm, relaxed, and happy:

- Just being - doing nothing on purpose
- Playing
- Enjoying nature
- Meditating
- Prayer
- Affirmations
- Gratitude
- Connecting with others
- Creating
- Setting intentions
- Learning
- Reading

- Journaling
- Letter-writing
- Doodling/drawing
- Singing
- Dancing
- Laughing
- Coloring
- Yoga/stretching
- Tree hugging
- Brushing animals
- Painting
- Drumming
- Swim/bathe/shower/skinny-dipping
- Daydreaming
- Listening
- Helping others
- Puzzling
- Laying or sitting in the grass (Earthing)
- Sitting near water
- Walking
- Noticing
- Photography
- Imagining
- Cloud/sun/moon/star/fire gazing
- Sending love to those who need it
- Finding joy in something simple

- Seeing through the eyes of a tourist

I suggest you make a list for yourself. It may start small and grow, like mine did. Mine started out with only *reading*, *writing*, and *painting*. Each time I did something that made me happy I added it to the list. It is still growing.

Notice that some of the things on my list seem ridiculous, frivolous, silly, or meaningless. Well, so what? Self-care is the meaning. When I paint for self-care I am not worried about the end product or some other outcome. I am only concerned about my enjoyment of the activity. That is why it is self-care. I am taking my inner child out to play.

Once you begin to know what makes you feel joyful and you have it written down, you may need to put it somewhere visible to remind yourself to do those things…as often as possible.

Notice how some of the things on my list can be done anywhere. Some can take all day and some only a few minutes. I realize now just how easy it is to show yourself love once you know what that looks like.

You Are Worthy, My Dear!

Do it for yourself. You deserve it. How do I know you deserve it? I just do! I may not know you personally, but I know you are a soul, just like me. I know that you were born into a body, just like me. I know that you have spent your whole life doing the best you could with what you had at the time, just like me. I know that you made mistakes, went through struggles, and would perhaps do some things differently if you could, just like me. We are all equally special, but in different ways. We all have something special to contribute and we all deserve great things.

We all can have it all and that doesn't take anything away from others. There is enough love and abundance in the Universe for everyone to have all of their wishes come true. We are all from the same Source, even though we may have different names for him/her/it. We are all loved and looked after by that Source and we are all deserving of love and grace and beauty and abundance. All equally.

CHAPTER **SIX**:
DREAMS MADE REAL

I invite you now to start Beanstalking with me! Let's make magic happen!

Manifesting

It is time to begin to manifest your visions. Manifesting is the practice of thinking aspirational thoughts with the purpose of making them real. The word *manifest* can mean "to display or show" or "to embody." I want to also explain how I define *manifesting*. I have had people become uncomfortable with that word so I will explain what I believe it is and what it is not.

Manifesting is not evil—in the context of Beanstalking it has nothing to do with ghosts or conjuring. It is not magic spells or witchcraft or manipulation or woo-woo. It is not worshiping some strange deity. It is not a way to get whatever you want, no matter what you want and with no regard for others. It is not instantaneous. It is not limited to only certain people. We all have the ability to bring great things into our lives.

Manifesting is believing and receiving what you desire by putting your clear wishes out into the Universe. It is, in my opinion, like prayer. You are setting a very clear intention about what you desire in your mind and heart and perhaps putting it on paper. Then you are asking a higher power (God, Source, the Universe) to bring it to be in your life and trusting that it will come. It is essentially very much like praying. The only difference—and depending on how you pray, there may be no difference—is that you backup your prayer with feelings and actions. I think of it as proactive prayer. After becoming clear about your goal and asking for it, you immediately become grateful for it and act as though it is already true. You demonstrate such faith that it will be true, that it becomes so. In this way you display, show, or embody what you desire. You act as though it is happening in the present tense. This sends a message out through energy that tells the Universe (God/Source) what to send back your way. Just asking is not enough. You must see it, believe it, and be grateful for it coming to you…even before it comes.

If you are always sending out negative vibes you will get back negativity. If you consistently send out good vibes, that is what you will get in return. It's not to say that bad things will never happen to you. Bad things happen to every human on Earth in some way or another. It means that you will experience more positivity if you are positive. Being positive does not mean avoiding or ignoring difficult emotions, either, but being positive will help you to cope with and/or learn from any difficulties that life brings.

Resistance

If you want something desperately and you are begging for it, longing for it, and wishing and hoping, you are sending out an energy of resistance. You are saying you *don't* have it, but you want it, so you are essentially saying, "I lack it." The Universe will send more of that (lack). If you send out a "Thank you for what you brought me" you are saying, "I have it," and the Universe will send that energy to you in return.

Think of a kid. You say to them, "Don't touch that," and the next thing they do is touch it. Our brains are funny that way. Try this: If I say "Whatever you do, do *not* think about a slice of pie." What did you do? You thought about a slice of pie...and then you tried to not think about it, or you pretended you weren't thinking about it, but the pie was planted in your brain and the *not* didn't have a chance.

So it is with the Universe. You must tell it what you want, not what you don't want. If you tell it what you don't want, expect to get exactly that.

What you resist, persists. I know that my biggest fear in life has always been losing one of my loved ones, specifically my husband or kids. I don't think *at all* that it was my fault that my husband died, but I can see, in hindsight, that if I could have just put all of the love energy that made me fear losing him into simply being deeply grateful for him, I would have been happier and more at ease while he was here. If I could have a re-do, I would do that.

Trying to control every bit of the who, what, when, and where of getting your desires is another form of resisting. You must make room for surprises, miracles, and magic to happen to allow great things to come to you. When you try to be in control of the outcome, you are limited to only what you can imagine, while what the Universe can deliver is infinite in its possibilities. Let go of the need to control. Open your heart and mind and allow for awesomeness!

Your Vision

In this chapter you will begin to create a vision of your desires. This is the time to have a Beanstalk Book (a sketchbook or journal), scissors, glue-stick, and magazines ready.

Take a look back at your inventory survey. Choose one area to work on to begin making your vision clear. Whichever area of your life you are most motivated to work on, really look at what you are happy about and what you are unsatisfied with. This could even be an area that you are already satisfied with but want to make it even better. This may be one that you are very unsatisfied with and really want to change. You decide what makes you happy as a starting place. Start with what you feel you can handle without getting overwhelmed.

Choosing a goal that takes lots of time to make happen (or much of what it takes to make it happen is out of your control) might not be the best choice to start with if you are an impatient person. I am not saying you can't start with that, but you may want to start smaller to get the feeling of progress and success before taking on something that will require lots of patience. You decide how big you want to dream. Some may want to start small or you may not want to waste another minute waiting and so go for the big dream first. Whatever your approach, know that it's ok. Do it your way. Once you have chosen the area to focus on, write out a clear goal/dream. Write this goal in the present tense as though it is already true for you.

If you do not have a clear goal, you may begin looking through magazines and find things that inspire you and help you work toward getting a clear goal in mind. As you clip things from magazines you can begin gluing them into your Beanstalk Book and make small vision boards on the pages. If it helps you to make a whole page for one goal then do that. I tend to have pages that are all about one goal, but sometimes I put all different goals intermingled on one page. You can do whatever feels good to you.

I want to remind you again that this does not have to look fancy or beautiful. If you practice perfectionism and nothing ever gets put in the book, you may really miss out on some of the miracles that could be in your life. Just get it in the book. As your pages come together you will be able to see more clearly what you desire and making a clear written goal will then be possible for you.

When you have your clear, written goal you can look at it and read it often, adding or subtracting things to make it exactly resonate with your whole being. You can write your goal in your Beanstalk Book or on a sticky note or somewhere you can see it and keep it near you.

Here is an exercise to help you develop a clear goal. It is a bit like story-stretchers I used to use for my students when teaching them to write. It begins with a simple sentence and then you add details. I'll give you a typical story-stretcher example. Notice that it starts out as a very simple thought and each new sentence adds more details, adjectives for visualization, as well as answering questions like who what, when, where, and why. The underlined words are the new detail added on each line.

I love rainbows.
I love rainbows <u>in the sky</u>.

I love <u>the magic of bright, colorful</u> rainbows in the sky.
I love the magic of bright, colorful rainbows in the sky <u>and the smell of the air after it rains.</u>
I love the magic of bright, colorful rainbows in the sky and the smell of the air after it rains <u>on a summer day</u>.
I love the magic of bright, colorful rainbows in the sky and the smell of the air after it rains on a summer day <u>because it reminds me of how beautiful life is.</u>

Now that you see the story stretcher concept in action we can use that to write a clear goal. This can be done in one sitting or you can write the first simple sentence and keep it out somewhere you can get to easily, along with a pen/pencil so you can add to it as the details come to you.

Here is a story stretcher example for manifesting a new job. *I want a new job*, could be your exasperated simple sentence, so let's go with that. You can think of what you say when you are feeling exasperated or when you feel like you are working against what your heart and soul needs. Listen to what you say in your head and out loud at times when you are overwhelmed. You will learn a lot from yourself.

I want a new job.

I want a new job <u>with better pay</u>.

I want a new job with better pay <u>and hours that allow for more time with my loved ones</u>.

I want a new job with better pay, <u>good benefits</u>, and hours that allow for more time with my loved ones.

I want a new job with better pay, good benefits, and hours <u>and weekends off</u> that allow for more time with my loved ones.

I want a new job with better pay, good benefits, <u>flexible hours,</u> and weekends off that allow for more time with my loved ones.

I want a new job <u>that allows me to use my problem-solving skills</u> with better pay, good benefits, flexible hours, and weekends off that allow for more time with my loved ones.

I want a new job that allows me to use my problem-solving skills, <u>and work with strong leaders</u>; with better pay, good benefits, flexible hours and weekends off that allow for more time with my loved ones.

I want a new job <u>working for a local company</u> that allows me to use my problem-solving skills, and work with strong leaders; with better pay, good benefits, flexible hours, and weekends off that allow for more time with my loved ones.

I want a new job working for a local company that allows me to use my problem-solving skills, and work with strong leaders; <u>while spending at least part of my work week in the outdoors</u>; with better pay, good benefits, flexible hours, and weekends off that allow for more time with my loved ones.

<u>I want to be appreciated at</u> a new job working for

a local company that allows me to use my problem-solving skills, and work with strong leaders; while spending at least part of my work week in the outdoors; with better pay, good benefits, flexible hours and weekends off that allow for more time with my loved ones.

I want to be appreciated at a new job working for a local company <u>close to home</u> that allows me to use my problem-solving skills, and work with strong leaders ;while spending at least part of my work week in the outdoors ;with better pay, good benefits, flexible hours, and weekends off that allow for more time with my loved ones.

Once you have the details and criteria for your ideal job, you need to then (if you haven't already) put the dream in the present tense.

I am appreciated at my new job working for a local company close to home that allows me to use my problem-solving skills, and work with strong leaders; while spending at least part of my work week in the outdoors; with great pay, good benefits, flexible hours, and weekends off that allow for more time with my loved ones.

Write your story-stretched sentence on a sticky note and place it in your Beanstalk Book, on your mirror, refrigerator, night-stand, or anywhere you will see it and read it often. You now have a clear goal written in the present tense. If it continues to change as you realize what you desire then change it as you go. It will only help to make the visualization more clear and more real. Read it often. Daydream about it. Immerse yourself in the visualization and truly feel what it feels like for it to be reality.

Making the first vision page and/or writing down your clear vision is the first of many magic beans that you will plant. The beauty of magic beans is that you can plant as many as you like. You can even change your mind after planting one and plant a new one in its place, or let them both grow to see what happens. The possibilities are endless and the world has enough space for *all* of *everyone's* beanstalks!

What I mean by this is that if we all follow our dreams and work to make our hearts happy, there is enough room for everyone's happiness. When we wish for what our hearts want it may have something to do with money, but not usually money for money's sake. If everyone wished for all of the money in the world just so that we could say we had all of the money, it would not work out for anyone. That is not a goal that is for the highest and best good for anyone so it simply wouldn't happen. Our dreams can be grand without being greedy.

The *why* behind your dream is important. If your goal is for money or for a certain dollar amount, take a look at that goal. Stop and think about why you want the money. Is it to just get by, to erase fears of lack, or pay off debt, to pay for college, to invest in art classes, to nurture your inner passion, to learn a new skill that will benefit you? Or is it to look good to someone else, to have more than someone else? Dig deep and find out your *why*. When connecting to your *why* you become more passionate about your dream or it can make you refocus to a different, more deeply important goal for you.

When manifesting money for something specific, keep in mind that there are more ways than one to get things. I would recommend you be open to it appearing for you in ways other than just getting the money. If you want a new car, manifest a new car rather than the money for a car. If you want a trip, manifest the trip, not the money for the trip. In doing this you allow for more opportunities to come your way. You could win a car. You could be gifted a trip by someone who cannot use it. There are limitless possibilities for how it can come to you if you are open to them.

If we all wish for what makes us truly, intrinsically happy and for the abundance needed to make our wishes come true, there is more than enough love, abundance, and space for creativity for everyone.   It is possible for you to be extremely happy and satisfied with all of the areas of your life....a*ll the time*! Did you know that? I think I kind of thought there was some sort of rule that there has to be at least one part of our lives that isn't awesome. That is totally wrong. We can have 100% satisfaction in all areas of our lives. We can be happy with everything all of the time—or at least a majority of the time. I know life happens. Sometimes what it takes is to just get out of our own way! We need to stop believing in unwritten rules that make us think we are limited and have to follow a path that does not make us happy. Our limiting beliefs hold us back, keep us believing in scarcity, and make us fearful to try to make things different or better. Believe that your life can be enchanted and then truly it can be!

Be Clear and Specific

In a funny way, I learned a lesson about being clear and specific in asking for what I wanted. One dream that I was working on was helping to manifest a job with Apple Music Radio for my husband. He had a potential opportunity there and I wanted to help him make it happen so I began to make a page in my Beanstalk Book for him. I wasn't sure how to articulate the goal through magazine pictures so I started by finding Apple products like iPhones and MacBooks and devices I could find pictures of. Then I ran across the word *apple* and decided that I could probably find lots of pictures of apples so I made a whole page of collaged apples of many types.

A week or so later a neighbor, whom I had not met, came knocking on my door and introduced herself. She had a wagon full of pies. She told me she had just baked nine apple pies and wanted to share with others and did I want a pie? I smiled at the beautiful, neighborly gesture, thanked her, and happily took the pie. That same week I was driving past a different neighbor's house and she flagged me down and said, "Stay here a minute. I made applesauce and would like to give you some." I gladly took the sweet treat, smiled at my neighbor, and smiled a little on the inside. A couple of days later I had a friend bring me a whole bag of apples from her apple tree. She said she thought of me and wondered if I'd like them. I accepted them gratefully and laughed at the abundance of apples in my life and thought to myself, "Perhaps I need to be more specific!"

Here is my apple page:

I can pray for great things to happen to someone else, but I do not think I can manifest for them. The apples taught me that what I am drawing in will come to me and not to the other person.

Do not let this scare you though. You may unintentionally bring yourself an abundance of apples, but you won't manifest every thought that runs through your mind or every daydream you have. You will draw what you focus on and what is meant for you. Another way to be clear is to simply order what you want. It is like going to a restaurant. You sit down and browse the menu. You decide what you want and tell the wait staff what you desire. You then sit back and enjoy the ambiance and the company, and you relax into the event. You have confidence that the message about what you ordered will be delivered to the chef and that your order will be delivered to you. Manifesting is the same. You first become clear about your order, then you order it, and then you relax, trust, and believe it's coming. When the meal comes it may exceed your expectations and be the most beautiful plate arranged in a way you never dreamed possible. Be sure in manifesting that in the ordering you are specific about what you want…and that your order will reach the powers that be. Relax in knowing that what is meant for you will come. The timing and presentation is not yours to worry about. Just enjoy as you wait.

Commit

Once you figure out what you desire, commit to it. One thing I see very often is someone will say clearly what they want. They believe it will come and know it will be great and they press the gas pedal and charge full-speed ahead. Then things start happening, moving in the right direction, and they put on the brakes. Fear is making them doubt and they become scared of what may or may not happen and then they put on the brakes. Fear and doubt are normal things to think and feel, but we need to let those feelings flow through us and keep the foot on the gas, even if just gently.

Here is an example from when I was learning to ride a horse. My kids rode horses all of their lives and I was the mom in the stands watching them barrel race. I knew little or nothing about riding, only what I had heard while watching their years of lessons. When Wes and I were empty-nesters, we took lessons once a week so I could learn to ride. He came along for the extra practice and to enjoy time with me and with our great instructor. (A funny side note here: Wes used to leave work every Tuesday afternoon to do "a thing with my wife," as he told people at work. He was always vague about it and we laughed that his employees either thought we were in marriage counseling or had some kind of weekly afternoon delight. It makes me smile to think about it.) That barn where we took those lessons is where we gathered for Wes' celebration of life—with horses standing ready, in the dirt with the sweet smell of old leather in the air. Wes got a send-off he would have loved.

Anyway, back to one of the lessons that I learned in that barn while riding.

I was on the sweetest horse ever and she took good care of me. When given the right cue from her rider, she knew *exactly* what to do. I was just learning, so I was listening to all of the instructions: "Keep your hands forward, toes up, heels down, back relaxed, shoulders straight, chin up, eyes on where you are going. To make the horse go, gently squeeze your legs to the horse's sides." I would sit atop that horse and get situated and have all of that in place. I would signal her to walk. She would start walking and I would tense up—and consequently squeeze my legs harder around her, which meant go faster—and then she would go faster and I would feel out of control and panic and forget all the instructions and pull the reigns back to signal her to stop, while my legs had a death grip on her to tell her to go. The poor horse had no idea what I wanted from her. I was pushing the gas pedal and the brake at the same time. I remember the day I "got it" and we had a smooth ride as she understood what I wanted. It felt amazing.

I see people doing the same thing when committing to what they desire. Once there's forward motion they panic, second-guess, forget all instructions and signal a stop. Being aware of this is the best way to handle it. Once you can observe something in yourself, a behavior or fear, you then have the power to fix it.

Be clear that committing to something in this way does not commit you to the outcome. It's not like signing a contract. If you draw something to you and then change your mind about your desire, you will always and forever have free will to say no when it comes, or choose something different. Be sure that if you do say no when it comes to you, it is so you can pursue something better and not out of fear.

Intuition

Intuition is the immediate apprehension or power of knowing something without rational thought or inference. We all have intuition. Some people's intuition is highly developed while others rarely pay any attention to it. Whatever the case may be for you, the truth is we all have it.

We have gut feelings about things, some good feelings and some uneasy feelings about certain situations or people.

I suggest that you begin to take notice of your intuition. Notice when you get a feeling in your belly that something is off. Notice when you feel the energy of someone who is excited or happy near you. Becoming in tune with your intuition will help you as you begin to determine what you desire out of life.

Your intuition is connected to your heart and your gut. Use feelings there to help you decide when you are on the right path when you are choosing to partner with others for projects or get into relationships. Our intuition is such a useful tool when we learn how to listen for what it's telling us. Our minds are great at telling us how to get things done, but our intuition is what helps us to know what we want and to choose the direction. I highly recommend tuning in to what your body is telling you.

An example of noticing my intuition that you may relate to is that often a friend or family member will come to my mind. I will think of them and have an urge to text or call them out of the blue. When I follow through with the action attached to the feeling and reach out to them, so often I am told "I really needed to hear that today" or "I was just thinking about you."

Another example of following my intuition was when Layton and I were going camping a couple of summers ago. We set an intention to find the best camping spot, one with an amazing view and no other people. In midsummer near a national park, that was a tall order. We would be lucky to find *any* camping spot.

We were driving on a steep, narrow forest service road. We had been driving for quite some time and were hoping that it was leading to somewhere cool, but we honestly didn't know if it would suddenly end or loop back around or where it would lead us. The road was rough and we were starting to wonder if the truck with the slide-in camper could navigate any steeper or bigger bumps that may be ahead of us. Then we came to a fork in the road. We had to decide what to do. There was no room to turn around, but we had two possible directions to take.

We got out and each of us inspected one fork of the road. Neither looked better or worse than the other, but we couldn't tell where either of them led and we needed to make a decision. I told Layton that I had noticed a few miles back on the road there were two butterflies that seemed to be hanging around the windows and windshield, appearing and reappearing as we drove up the mountain. I asked him how he felt about following the butterflies. He said he was game. I pointed to the road going to the left and said "They went that way."

So we got back in the truck and followed that road (and the butterflies) and ended up on the top of the mountain in *the most* beautiful campsite! We were the only people around and we had a majestic view of the Teton Mountains. It was an incredible camping experience.

Our magical camping spot with the perfect view of the mountains and a photo of Boone and me on a walk near our campsite.

The more I follow my intuition, the more I trust it and don't hesitate when I get inner nudges. Listening to your intuition, staying in touch with your gut, is a wonderful way to stay true to yourself, and a beautiful part of being human.

Be Open

Being open to great things is important. It is important if you have a clear and specific goal because *how* things happen is not really your concern. Sure, you can do things to get yourself closer to your goal, and you can see the outcome you want, but you must be open to the magic and miracles that will surpass your wildest imagination. If you are not, you are really limiting yourself when the possibilities are limitless. It is so much more fun to see how the Universe works it out in magical ways than it is to plan it and implement the plan. Being open when you do not have a clear goal is also helpful in creating your vision. It can help you to begin to see the path that is right for you.

Here is an example from my journey of being open:

While Wes was still here, I could clearly see the path in front of us. I knew exactly what our future held, or so I thought. We were going to travel and go on adventures, then we were going to retire and travel some more, and then watch our children get married, enjoy our grandkids, grow old together, and love each other forever. I saw that in my mind as a road—going straight ahead with some curves and hills, full of wonder and beauty all around. When he passed away it was as if that road had been completely destroyed by some force of nature—like a flood washed it away or an earthquake disrupted the land and distorted it beyond recognition. That road was not just closed, it was gone forever. That was a real image in my mind.

At some point during my healing I remember letting go of the image of the road and the destruction of the unpassable path. I remember switching that image into a peaceful lush meadow. I sat in the meadow in my mind and looked out at the grass and flowers and trees in the distance, wondering where I was headed. There were no roads, paths, or trails to be seen. Wes was not by my side, at least not in the physical form. I then extended my arms out in a gesture of opening. My prayer was this: *I see no path in front of me. I do not know where to go. Take me wherever I am meant to be. Use me as I am needed. Help me to create my own path from here to where you need me to go. I surrender and am open to new possibilities.*

After that experience I felt lighter about not knowing where I was headed. I knew that I would be guided and, if I listened and noticed the signs and clues, I would find my way.

I became a super-noticer, seeing signs and wonders all around me, everywhere. It was a magical awakening. I was open to any and all signs, information and ideas coming my way. I frantically cut and pasted ideas into my Beanstalk Book and looked for ways I could find my purpose and truly discover what my heart was longing for.

I encourage you to do the same. Be open and allow for things to come to you while you search out and draw in the things you already know you want.

CHAPTER **SEVEN**:
FEARS AND OBSTACLES

Fear

Have you ever said the words, "I have always wanted to___, but ___"? For my whole life I have said I wanted to learn to swim. I still do not know how to, really. The longer I go not knowing how to swim, the more excuses I make about why I never will. The only reason for me not learning as an adult is fear. I hear the same from others so often too. I have heard things like, "I always wanted to… write a book, travel abroad, befriend an elderly person, swim with the dolphins, paint, ski, climb a mountain, learn a new skill, start my own business, see something amazing, create something beautiful, change careers, learn to belly-dance, do something great. So many wishes halted—some by real or perceived obstacles, some by finances, but many by fear.

Fear can be such a debilitating force. I am working very hard in my life to not make decisions based on fear, because fear will almost always hold us back. Fear was designed within us to protect us (to alert us to be afraid if we are about to fall off a cliff, or to stop us from playing with fire, or to prompt us to run from a predator), but it has become a factor for making everyday decisions and keeping us from doing what our hearts desire.

I do believe in listening to my gut when I feel threatened or am in a scary situation. This is fear doing its job.

I do not believe in letting fear stop me from asking for what I need or want. Believe me that this has been a chore for me. I spent many years not doing things because I was afraid. I was afraid of how it would make me look to others. I was afraid of disappointing others, afraid of looking selfish, looking crazy, looking stupid, making a fool of myself. I was afraid to be vulnerable. I now realize I need to be vulnerable and face my fears so that I can do what makes me happy. I have always feared that people would judge me. Well, I now know that, yes, they will. No matter what I do, there is a possibility that someone will judge me. That is neither my problem nor my business. My job is to keep myself happy. I am getting better at this everyday.

I never want to get so good at making myself happy that I don't respect others and their opinions (when appropriate), as relationships are extremely important to me. I just don't want the fear of the opinions of others to be my guide for deciding my own future and happiness.

If I'm making a decision and I feel fear, I try to listen to it. I talk to it—I know that sounds crazy, but hear me out. I ask the fear for an explanation: "What are you afraid of?" I write down what comes to me. The answers are very telling.

For example, if the fear says:

- "I am afraid that getting that new big dream house will mean I have to move and give up my old place and pack all of those boxes and ask for help and all of the hard parts of moving," that is fear trying to protect you from doing some temporary hard work, and actually limiting you from having your dream home.

- "I am afraid of changing jobs, because what if I don't like the new place or the co-workers or what if it's worse than the job I have now?" the "what if" is a big sign that fear is trying to protect you but is coming up short so is making things up to protect you from something imaginary. This fear is limiting you. "What if" it's your dream job?

Some ways to help your fear calm down are to:

- Make a pros-and-cons list and let your heart fill out the pros and your fear fill out the cons.

- Imagine each item on the list for two minutes each. Fully imagine—immerse yourself into what it feels like to do one of those choices, and then fully live into the other ones. Which ones made your heart happier?

- Find a "Whatif Wizard" (read on)…

There is a wonderful children's book called *Jonathan James and The Whatif Monster*, by Michelle Nelson-Schmidt. It is about a monster who takes away all your bad "whatifs" and leaves you with only the exciting and beautiful possibilities—the good whatifs. I once told my students that I was afraid to try something new and, unsolicited, one sweet first-grade girl (a little, blond, bobbed-hair, and blue-eyed, front-teeth-missing girl named Lily) raised her hand and said, "Mrs. Nussbaum, I'll be your whatif monster." When a child does a kind, brave, and beautiful act like that, you go with it! So I told her all the reasons I was afraid to do something new (she gobbled them up) and the class and I then discussed all of the awesome reasons why I should be excited to try! It was a genuine and spontaneous moment in my classroom and I knew that I had no reason to not try painting dog pictures so I did….and I *loved* it!

That book inspired me to make a Whatif Wizard who waves a wand and magically takes away all of the doubt/fear/bad whatifs. Anyone who loves you and wants to see you happy and successful can be your Whatif Wizard… and you don't have to call them that, just a good friend doing what friends do is fine, but I rather like the title.

Another way to help fears calm down is to:

• Ask for divine guidance. Ask for a sign or a sense of knowing.

I experienced so much fear when I was faced with opening my heart up to love. I had, months prior, gotten a message from Wes in spirit that said he was pulling strings and bringing love to me. He said, "Please do not turn away from it because of me. You loving again takes nothing away from our love." I cried and did not want to hear that I would ever love again. I did not want that.

When I was faced with the opportunity and there was a man who made me laugh and understood my journey, I was terrified! FEAR, not with a capital F, but ALL CAPS! I did not know what to do. I knew that I was at that place that Wes had talked about—potential love in front of me. *Do I turn away?*

I asked for divine guidance. I prayed and asked for a sign. If saying yes to that relationship was part of my highest and best path, I asked specifically to be shown a license plate with the numbers 528 on it. I chose 528 because I'd learned on my journey to self-love that in the ancient solfeggio frequencies 528 hertz is known as the frequency of love. Within a day or two of asking for the sign, I was out shopping with my friend and I saw a car just outside the store, on the sidewalk near the door, instead of in the parking lot. I noticed the car because it was in the way. Then I noticed the license plate and saw it was from Hawaii, which is only a million miles away across an ocean, a place where Wes and I once vacationed, so I was distracted by that for an instant, and then I noticed those digits: FIVE-TWO-EIGHT! I gasped, stopped breathing for a second, and snapped a picture (partly because I take pictures of everything, and partly to make sure it was real… sometimes when crazy things happen I almost don't believe it or I doubt myself and what I saw or heard). Then I totally freaked out on the inside! I tried to be calm with my friend and simply said I had asked for a sign and gotten one. I cried and panicked most of the rest of the day!

Here is the photo:

After I recovered from the shock and the understanding of the answer I'd just received, I was then faced with what to do with the information. I certainly had the choice to move forward or stay put. I remember being in my "nest," a comfy chair where I usually sat to do my reading, writing, meditating, crying, talking on the phone—ya know, my spot—and hearing a voice within my own self, perhaps my voice or perhaps not my voice, I honestly do not know, but I very clearly heard a calm and strong voice. The voice said, "You can sit here and continue to be sad or you can get up and live." At that moment I decided to live. I decided to face my fear and allow the relationship into my life and see where it might go.

One thing to remember is that you always have the choice. When you ask for guidance and receive it, you still have the power to choose it or not. If something comes to you that you thought you wanted, but you decide you don't, you aren't obligated. We will forever have free will. Be careful not to reject based on fear, though. I am so glad I chose to stand up to my fear and let love in. If something great comes to you, I hope you know that you deserve it, allow yourself to grab it, love it, and feel grateful that life is bringing you happiness.

As I have helped others make their own Beanstalk Books I have noticed that while cutting things out of magazines they are open and excited and allowing themselves to dream and hope and wish. They are usually having a big time! Then when it comes to actually placing them in the book they begin to "think" too much and it drains all of the fun out. Pasting is the point when people experience the most fear. First, some get caught up in the placement of things—and again, it doesn't matter what it looks like. Then people will begin to question: *Does putting it in the book automatically make it so? Does this mean I am committed to this new thing? What if it doesn't come true? Or, even scarier, what if it does come true?* Fear is normal when we're presented with change. Just because it is normal, however, does not mean it is the feeling we should let override the fun and excitement of greatness coming to us.

Here is an example of when fear came up for me in that way.

Let me be very clear that after Wes died I was not looking for a man, not ever wanting to give or receive that kind of love again. I certainly did not set out to find a guitar-playing man. But one day, while cutting things from magazines, I happily ripped out a page of the magazine with the image of a man playing guitar (shown in the Introduction). When I cut that out of the magazine, I was simply doing as I had been taught: If it resonates or speaks to me in some way, cut it out. I did that. I did not understand it. I did not play guitar. I did not want to learn to play guitar. I resolutely *did not* want a man. But the image stirred a feeling in me, so I ripped it out and put it aside.

Later, as I was pasting things into my book, I came across that image of the guitar man. I didn't understand why I had clipped it from the magazine. Frankly, it then made me uncomfortable. I swiftly hid that picture on the bottom of a pile, to deal with…well, perhaps never.

It wasn't until sometime later, after I had accepted the idea of opening my heart and welcomed a new relationship, that I went through my "to be glued pile" and found, on the bottom of the pile, the guitar-man picture.

Even after making the connection that the man I had started seeing was a professional musician, I struggled to have the courage to glue it in my book. *Is this what my heart wants even though my brain and all of the rest of me is vehemently opposed?* I was a bit terrified at the power of what was happening. Terrified and perplexed and fascinated and excited.

It wasn't until I surrendered to the relationship and actually opened my heart to love again that I finally put it in my dream book. It was scary.

Just because things are scary does not mean they are wrong for us. So many of life's greatest times are, in fact, very scary. Getting married is scary, having a baby, moving, buying a big-ticket item, traveling to a new place, meeting new people, getting a dog or cat, writing a book, singing in front of others...can all be scary, but they all can be amazing. Fear has its place, but not in determining your future!

Here's another layer of greatness that came into my life through the pictures and words in my Beanstalk Book: I have a magazine clipping of a man playing guitar and my new husband plays guitar as a profession. All of what I said about being heartbroken over the death of my husband is truth. The other truth is that love can happen again. Love will always continue to happen. We are made for love.

Layton and I both feel like when we married our young loves we *hit the jackpot*! We each had a wonderfully loving and long marriage and a beautiful life and family with our soulmates. We now have a second chance to continue to grow in love with each other after our losses. We call this part of our lives *the bonus round*! We agree there is a magical connection between us. We have another opportunity to live and love and share all of the joys life has to offer and we feel like we can't lose, because we have both already won, *twice*!

So many things—amazing, profound, simple, and magical things have happened in my life that were in my dream book. I honestly wouldn't believe it myself if I didn't have the proof.

Judgment

We have been programmed our whole lives to judge everything. It is how we are taught to choose right from wrong and make "good choices." I am not saying this is a good or bad thing, it just is. We are taught to think before we speak or act, so we don't hurt others or get into trouble. We get so good at it that we let our power of discernment do all of our bidding, which leads to judging our own choices, our own wishes, dreams, and desires. When we judge ourselves like that, we hold ourselves back.

I was having lunch with my daughters and granddaughter just the other day. My granddaughter, who is 15 months old, is on the cusp of talking, but there is no doubt she clearly communicates. She uses nodding, pointing, reaching for objects, and some sign language to tell those around her what she wants. Oh my goodness, if you ever see a baby sign the word *please*, I promise you will give them whatever they want...Gah!! It's too adorable to resist! She clearly communicates what she doesn't want through shaking her head, turning her head away, saying no, arching her back, pushing things away, or crying. Watching her at lunch was so fascinating because she was so confident in what she wanted and she communicated her desires so simply and clearly. All of what she asked for was reasonable, so she got everything she wanted (water, bread, meat, cheese).

My daughters and I talked about how cool it is to see that she knows what she wants already. We talked about how we struggle sometimes with even the simplest decisions, as adults. The reason we struggle is this: We judge every thought that comes to mind. Using the example of the baby at lunch: She wanted water, meat, cheese, and bread; as adults we think *meat (I shouldn't have that—meat, is too high in fat, I should choose something better for me or I shouldn't want that* or *I shouldn't eat meat)*, cheese (*delicious, but oh the fat, so I shouldn't*), and bread…(*the gluten, the carbs…I shouldn't*). The only good choice then would be the water, and then it's, *Should I spend money on a bottle of water (the plastic)* or *Maybe I should get a cup and fill it for free, but then I'll want a straw.* See how our minds, which were programmed to keep us out of trouble, are now working against us? I am not saying we should make bad choices. I am saying that we need to give our minds a rest and not put a judgment on all of our thoughts. Allow for being, hoping, and dreaming, wishing, and desiring…at least long enough to discover what it is you want.

Let's attempt to think like children who want what they want.

Children want to be astronauts and professional ball players, dancers, artists, and rock stars. When they are small it's easy to allow them to dream those fanciful dreams. When they turn 18 and it's time to make it happen, we say, "Be a doctor, a lawyer, an accountant, or something more important or more lucrative or, at the very least, more practical." We are not trying to squash their dreams, but we judge and fear that they won't make it, or we fear that they won't have enough money to survive. Our fear encourages them to pursue something practical instead of something fanciful. There is an amazing song that says it perfectly. I consider it my anthem. Check out the song called *Daydream* by Lily Meola.

Comfort Zone

I know how much we all like comfort. We like to know we are safe and have all of our needs met. We know what to expect, good and bad. The consistency and predictability makes us feel safe…comfortable. The easiest way to get that is to stay put when we find comfort. If that is where you would like to be, that is a fine place. There is another place you could be, though. It is the bliss zone. This is the place where, once you get there, you not only have comfort, you have true happiness. Getting from the comfort zone to the bliss zone takes a few things: hope, courage, bravery, and risk. Yes, you risk losing things. You risk giving up what you have in hope for what you really want. You risk failing and you risk upsetting others, but to pursue what your heart desires and get it, it is worth it. No rewards come without risk. When you do what it takes to make greatness happen, great things can happen. If you do nothing to work toward greatness, things will never be more than good.

People Around You

You making changes will likely make others uncomfortable. It may make those who love you (family and friends) fear that you are taking a risk. They truly want what's best for you. They mean well, but they are attempting to set limits on your life based on their fear (on your behalf) when they express their opinions. Co-workers, peers, or even some friends may become uncomfortable because you are being bold and moving forward (they secretly want the same but are afraid to go for it), so they discourage you from following your dreams so they will feel better about not following theirs and they may not even be doing it consciously. Some of them may even attempt to sabotage your efforts on purpose. They simply cannot handle your growth and success.

What I suggest you do about the nay-sayers is to send them love. Smile. Carry on and do what is best for you. Sometimes encouraging them to also dream big and follow their hearts can dissipate the problems. Show them your Beanstalk Book and let them see that happiness is meant for all of us. They can do it too.

Life is a race and a competition to so many people. It is all they have ever known—trying to be the best, smartest, fastest, prettiest, etc. But if it is happiness we are pursuing, no one has to be the best at it. It is not a competition. There may be times when we are competing for the same position or possession, but truly we can all be happy and one person's happiness doesn't take away from another's. In fact, the opposite is true. One person's happiness can rub off on or inspire another's. People who truly love and support you will be there for you and with you and will want for you what you want for yourself. Find those people and share your joy and successes with them. When you find the right people they will also be the ones who are honest with you to help keep you on track. You can bounce ideas off of them and talk about your dreams and they will help you know which ones are worth following.

I have been so incredibly blessed to be surrounded by mostly very supportive people who just want me to be happy. I am grateful for them. The ones who have been less than supportive have also taught me something. They have taught me how to be a better friend and cheerleader. They have taught me to not judge the journeys of others, because we don't know what others are going through, and they have taught me to be kind and patient to the nay-sayers because they may be riddled with fear themselves. It reminds me that we, as temporary inhabitants of Earth, are really all on the same team and should be loving and compassionate toward all other inhabitants while we are here on this planet.

Start Small

The beautiful thing about this Beanstalking process is that you get to go at your own pace. There is no right or wrong. If you see or feel an area in your life that you would like to be happier with, start by identifying what you don't like, then switch the wording to what you would like. Then work toward changing that area.

The wonderful thing is that while you may think that making changes is hard, sometimes it is as simple as identifying the areas that need changing. I have worked with several people wanting a change in work. The first thing I tell them is to make a list of everything they would want their work to look and feel like. Do they want to work with people or independently, inside or outside, be challenged or creative or have a specific routine? I have them list everything they want to see in their job. The most amazing things have happened by making that list. They then know what they want and when the right job comes along they are instantly able to compare the job opportunity to their list and identify if it is the right one. Some have even seen natural changes in their current jobs that made them a closer match to their lists—just by identifying it was what they wanted and then recognizing how the company restructure moved them to a different team of people or to a division where the work was more suited to their desires. It truly is amazing to watch those things happen to people and to watch others get closer to living their enchanted life, just by making simple changes in thoughts and actions.

When Beanstalking we are letting our hearts out to play and reaping the benefits as our reality aligns with our desires. The process of dreaming does not have to start with big changes. You may start with simply wanting to find the right sofa or light fixture. Dip your toe in the water first and see how it feels. Then dare to dream bigger. Get comfortable with the process before you get serious about changes, if that works for you. Just start. Your future self will thank you! I am giving you permission to dive right in, though, if you are one who needs to jump in all at once instead of getting used to the water bit by bit. I am one who gets in and dunks under right away instead of prolonging the hard part of slowly acclimating.

Understand that as your dreams get bigger and more clear, there may be stepping stones. If you are looking for a person who is your soulmate, a forever home, a best friend, or new job and you clearly put your intentions into your book and in your heart and mind, the first one you come across may not necessarily be the one you're looking for. People, things, and situations will be drawn to you. The new job you are offered may or may not be your dream job; it may be a stepping stone to your dream job, or it may be a great job, but not the job you were hoping for. Try to keep these things in mind as you see good things coming your way.

Sometimes there are things put in your path to prepare you for the real thing. A friend once was hurting from a past relationship. She had lost all hope in ever finding love and, honestly, even wanting to. She was set on refusing all love interests or situations—pretty much warding off men. She then began Beanstalking and realized that she wanted to travel and share her experiences with someone. That tiny magic bean began to germinate. She came to know a sweet and kind, fun and funny man. He was not "the one" for her, but he was put in her path to create a spark, a renewed hope and interest in the beautiful possibilities of love. She now has a list of what her future person will be and she will surely recognize him when he arrives.

Another friend is on a journey to her best life and is looking to find strong and lasting friendships. She has begun to join clubs, get out and do the activities she loves and meet people with common interests. Her first experience, however, was upsetting because she assumed that the first book club she joined was going to be the one where "her people" were. Having that expectation was wonderful and positive, but it set her up to feel like it was a failure when things didn't go as planned. That was one of those times when we have to sit back and relax into it. The first club may not be the place, but it may be the connecting piece of the puzzle that leads to the next piece or pieces falling into place naturally. It may also just have been a place where lovely people gathered, but not the people she was looking for, and so it was a place she could check off of her list of where to find what she desired. No harm done.

Remain open-minded and open-hearted and let things happen organically. Remember that the more we force and try to take control, the more we are resisting. Asking for divine guidance when you are not sure, can help you discern your highest and best path. *Is this is the dream being delivered, part of the path leading to the dream, or just a place you are passing by?* Be open to recognizing that all parts of the journey can be beautiful and carry lessons.

Challenges/Obstacles

Once we have things falling into place for us we may think we have made it and we can now manifest anything we want and life will be a breeze. Well, by definition, life is not a breeze. Life is for learning. I have always told my students that. We are here on Earth to learn. Everyday we wake up and learn—for our whole lives. Part of learning is growing, and growing is painful.

Layton and I had been married for nine months, living in our dream home for six months and we were both pursuing our passions and living our best life. Layton, while on a business trip, had a massive heart attack. He nearly didn't make it. Thankfully he was in Nashville with family at the time, as our rural area would not have had the immediate medical care that he needed to survive. He did survive and is doing well now. One thing that happened to us both after the heart attack was that we felt that all we were working toward was derailed, and we questioned our future goals.

With encouragement from others we realized that it was just a growth spurt. Layton was recovering well and had a new lease on life. We both had already lost our previous spouses, so we don't take one another for granted, but that was another wake-up call to make sure we never do! Life is precious and short. We also were reminded that life happens and we can overcome obstacles. Traumatic events can feel debilitating but when we allow space for grieving, processing our feelings, and learning (if there are any lessons in it), we can survive and still thrive afterward.

A lesson I continue to learn is that it is ok to ask for help. I feel like the Universe is going to keep giving me opportunities to learn this until I really get it. I will attempt to learn it in times of ease, so that I will not need any more large opportunities to ask for help, thank you very much!

I can see now that Layton's heart attack was not meant to stop us from following our dreams, but to help us gain even clearer focus on them.

Let nothing stop you from working toward your dreams.

CHAPTER EIGHT:
NEXT LEVEL

The Beanstalk Process is the reason you picked up this book. Here's how it works...

Cut It Out

Deciding what you want is the first step to getting it. Sometimes when we discover what it is we want we think it may be frivolous or pointless when, in fact, what we want is who we are, and we must honor that. We must honor who we are and live into our best selves to be truly happy.

It is not selfish to do what makes you happy. It will benefit everyone around you when you are true to yourself. Your happiness can help others find their happiness too. Make an effort to put *you* on your priority list. In the Beanstalking Process this is looking through magazines for what you desire and cutting out the things that resonate with you. If it makes your heart sing, cut it out to put in your book.

This part is called *dreaming it*. This is letting your heart lead you and is done rather unconsciously or subconsciously. It requires little thinking and lots of feeling and intuition. It's the good kind of feeling. It's dreaming up your best life. It is a call from your heart to unlock a part of you that is currently hidden away. It is expansive and light and feels fantastic. All of those bits and pieces cut out of magazines are your very own, personal, magic beans.

I am a true paper and pencil person, old school, get-my-hands-on-things kind of person, but you can do this digitally if you prefer. To do it digitally, have either an album for photos on your phone titled "Beanstalking" and gather photos from online and save them there, or use Pinterest or another app and create a Beanstalking board.

Paste It In

The next step is to look at something you've cut out and feel into it, believe it, and feel gratitude. Gratitude! Gratitude! Gratitude! Then paste the items cut from magazines into your Beanstalk Book. When doing this, consciously think about your dreams coming true. This requires your full attention. The attention is not on the placement of the pictures on the page—we know that doesn't matter. Put your attention on how it feels to have that thing in your life now. How it feels for that to come true for you right now. This is feeling how it feels to live your dream in the present moment. It requires that you believe (or begin to believe) that it is on its way for you. The best way to get there is to feel grateful for having received it already. When doing this it may spontaneously make you feel exhilarated and excited. It should. It's the beginning of amazing things for you. You have just planted your magic beans.

Those excited feelings are what it feels like to vibe high. When you are vibing high, the energy in your body is actually vibrating at a high frequency. Those are the ideal conditions for drawing to you what you most desire out of life. Your goal is to keep your vibration up as high as you can as much of the time as you can. To keep yourself at a high vibration, you can refer back to the list of things you do to make yourself happy. No one vibrates high all of the time, but that certainly is a fantastic goal. When you feel tired, sad, guilty, lonely, or ashamed you are vibrating at a low frequency. Not only does it feel terrible to be at that frequency, but when you vibe low you attract things and people to you that are of a lower vibration. Listening to high vibrational music is the fastest way to get back to vibing high for me.

I am not telling you to ignore your feelings. I am telling you to feel them and let them flow through you. As you do that you release them and are able to get back to a happy state faster than if you sit with them and return to them and allow them to stick around and keep you down. This may take a few minutes, an hour, a day, a week, or more, depending on the situation, but the goal is to return to feeling great, not to get used to feeling merely ok.

Keep It Together

I find that, with most everything in life, having a simple system to keep organized is helpful. I find that keeping Beanstalking simple so that it doesn't take too much time or effort to get it out, put it away, or to work on it makes it more likely to get done more often. It doesn't take much room, just any table or work surface will do. Having a trash or recycle bin nearby is helpful for the magazine clippings.

I have a Beanstalking Kit so that I always have the supplies I need to use in one spot. I also take it with me to Beanstalk with my soul-sister, my daughters, groups of people, or to the cabin, so having a portable container is perfect for me. I have all of my supplies (Beanstalk Book, magazines, scissors, glue stick, something to write with for making notes, a couple of gallon or quart-sized zipper bags for storing pieces I've cut out but not pasted yet)—all of it in a small vintage, suitcase. I like the suitcase because it looks nice sitting out in my studio, it is easy to grab, it has interior pockets for small items, and has a handle for carrying. My daughters each have a small canvas tote bag with their Beanstalking supplies, and a friend has a decorative box. You could easily use a drawer if you only work on it at home. Any container that suits you will work fine.

Check Back In

Looking at your Beanstalk Book pages full of picture goals on a regular basis is a good idea. Thumb through to see how things are growing, just as you would if you'd planted a seed in a pot or in the ground. You would check in on it periodically and see if it needed more light, water, food, kind words, or a change in conditions to keep it alive.

One friend wasn't sure where to store her Beanstalk Book and decided to keep it somewhere near her workspace so she could refer back to it. She called me to express her excitement about that decision after being confronted with someone questioning her dreams and pursuits of happiness. Doubt entered her mind. "Maybe they are right," she thought. She caught a glimpse of her vision book, picked it up and remembered her *why*. She used her Beanstalk Book to get back to center, find her true north and ignore the nay-sayer.

As you look through what you have done in your book, you may see things that have sprouted already. You may see no progress, but checking back in can help to renew the excitement and perhaps remind you to update that resume or make that phone call or pick out the paint color needed for the next step for a dream to come true. Great things will come to you but you still have to do some leg-work.

I wanted to find our dream home and it did come to us, but I had to look at homes that were for sale so that the right home could be put in our path. The Universe is magical, for sure, but we have to still participate in the regular societal norms to get to our dreams. You can use that review time to feel the high vibe dream again or to feel it more intensely. Send more gratitude. Being grateful for what is coming your way demonstrates your faith that it will happen. It is happening. There are things happening under the soil that you cannot see when a bean germinates and sprouts, just as there are things happening behind the scenes in your life that you cannot yet see until the time is right.

Grab The Goods

Be ready for it when it comes. You have done all the work to get to the point to see your beanstalk grow (a new career path as an artist) and thrive (submitting your artwork to a gallery) and reach for the sky (sharing your work with the world in a gallery). When the last or best bit of the dream comes true, be sure that you are there and ready and grateful. Sometimes even as things are going incredibly well we get in our own way of happiness and success. Be sure that you are doing your self-care so that you see your worth and know that you deserve it. Be sure that you are vibing high like when you planted the bean to begin with. Try to be in the same energetic space as you were when you dreamed your dream. Keep yourself from feeling doubt or getting impatient and frustrated if things don't happen at your preferred pace.

Here is a drawing to explain what I mean more clearly...this was adapted from something I read years ago, perhaps from Glennon Doyle. I would love to give proper credit where credit is due, but I cannot remember some of the details of things from the time I was deep in grief.

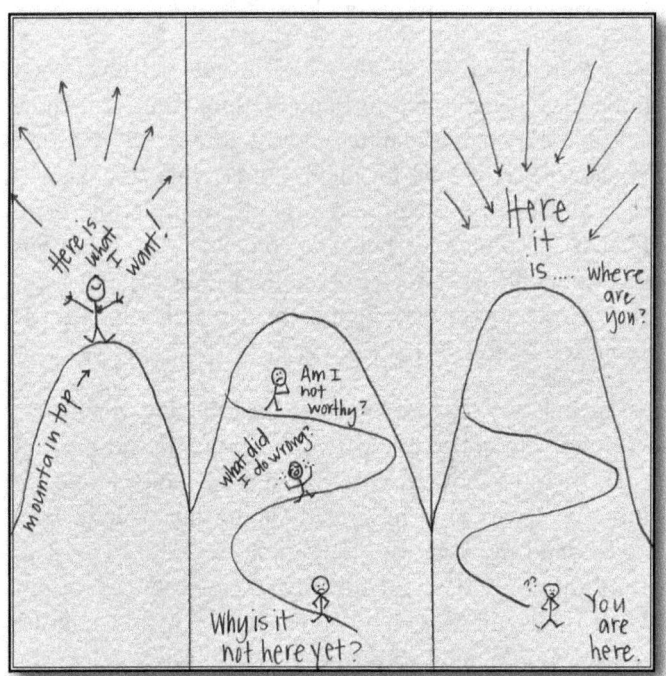

Keep an Eye Out

As I continued on my journey I was forever on the lookout for signs and wonders from beyond to help guide me on my way. You can think of these as breadcrumbs to help you find the way to what is meant for you. You can think of them as serendipities, *Godwinks* if you like or I have heard the term *tender mercies*. These beautiful clues help in so many ways. It is magical to know that you can ask for and receive signs to help you on your way.

I feel so much stronger and at peace knowing that I am not alone on my journey and that I don't have to guess my way through life. I have God, loved ones, guides, and angels who all are there to help me find my way. No matter how hard it gets, I am never alone.

I tell many stories of the ways in which I have been guided to where I am, and people think I am somehow special for receiving so many signs. I am special because I look for the signs. I ask for them, I notice them, I acknowledge and believe them, and I send gratitude for them. That is the difference between someone who gets signs and someone who does not: noticing and acknowledging them. I do not believe in coincidence. I believe those things to be signs.

The first time I asked for a sign was one day when I was writing in my journal and I was distraught and deep in grief. I wrote a note to Wes that said, "If you can see me and you approve of how I am doing life without you, please send me a giraffe." I then closed the journal and went about my day, not thinking about what I had just written. I live in Montana. Where would he find a giraffe to send me? What a strange request. I have no idea why I even picked a giraffe. It was spontaneous and held no meaning for me in any way.

Later that day I was on Instagram and I was attempting to click on something and I accidentally clicked on a different link...and it ended up being a giraffe. I was a bit surprised and told my daughters what I had asked of their dad, asked if they thought this counted. They said, "Yes!" I argued, "But your dad didn't even know how to use Instagram!" I couldn't really believe it was true.

Later that day my girls and I were driving across town and I was sitting in the backseat gazing out the window. To my surprise I spotted a giant, stuffed giraffe standing in a parking lot outside of an apartment building (apartment number 2,…so there was a 2 above the door and a 2 on the door so there was a giraffe and the number 22). I grabbed my phone to get visual proof that I was not seeing things and I noticed it was 4:22pm. I was convinced Wes was with us and could see us and approved of how I was doing.

So many emotions flooded through me at that moment. The best of them was love from above. Well, throughout that very day I saw five giraffes in different forms and places (note that this was years ago, before giraffes became an "in" thing that we see everywhere now) and I got the most clear and perfect message of my life. I was so grateful and I was sure then that I could ask for and receive signs when I needed them.

This is the actual photo I snapped that day.
I wasn't thinking clearly enough to get the apartment number in the picture.

Do It Again

Once one goal is accomplished or once a task is completed, repeat the process of returning to your life satisfaction survey, making updates to it and turning your focus to another goal, wish, or dream. As you continue to do this, your Beanstalk Book will fill up and so will your life. You do not actually have to do this linearly and wait for one goal to be accomplished before planting your next bean. You may have lots of beans planted and in different stages of growth at all times. The choice is yours. Do what feels right to you.

I feel such a sense of excitement when I am cutting things from magazines. Remember how I said that the guitar player scared me and now I am married to a guitar player? Well, now when I cut something out that I don't understand or has no actual "place" in my life, I am secretly tickled and curious about what my future holds and where this might fit in. I love thinking about the magic and infinite possibilities that are available to me.

An example of this is in my second 210-page sketch-book (Beanstalk Book volume 2). I keep finding myself putting in photos of stacks and stacks of books and bookshelves and home libraries. I currently have no room in my life or anywhere in my home for a library, but clearly it makes my heart happy to be surrounded by books. I like to entertain the possible secrets that this tells about my future. Is there another or a different home waiting for me? Will I spend my time in libraries or bookstores? Or perhaps find a way to live amongst books in the home and surroundings I have now. Maybe it's a metaphor and it symbolizes the future I have as a writer. I have no idea, but it excites me to think of what life has in store for me. If I stay out of my own way, I may get to experience this dream one day too!

The process of Beanstalking started for me at a time when I was focusing on pure survival. I have discovered that Beanstalking is a process that I will continue to use for the rest of my life. As I reach my goals, I make new ones. Each new goal becomes bigger and more beautiful as I realize that the possibilities are endless and I never have to stop learning and growing and being the best I can be! I feel like am walking through a magical forest of beanstalks that I have planted on my own and that I trusted the Universe, God, Wes, myself, and my spirit team to help grow for me. I will continue to water those dreams I have grown. I will tend to those that are newly planted. And I will joyfully plant all of the dreams that are still in the form of beans in my hand.

As you continue to watch wonderful things happen in your life, from loving yourself more and being present more often, to accepting the great gifts the Universe offers you remember that the best way to manifest abundance is to be grateful for all that you already have. Be honest with yourself. Be kind to yourself. Let yourself be happy.

The power to change, fix, release, or enhance any part of your life is within you. Step into your power and use the tools in this book to wave your magic wand to make miracles happen in and around you.

As you see how the process works for you, you can adjust your style of making your book. You can assess how things are working and not working and learn and grow from the process. You can learn about yourself and what makes you truly happy, and learn about your motivation and your manifesting style.

Remember to go back through the process and understand that this is more than just cutting and pasting. You are making your dreams come true. You are listening to your innermost wants and needs and making them happen in your life.

The most important of all things you can create in your own life is self-love which will lead you to inner peace.

The more peace you have within yourself, the more peace and love you can give to the world. You owe it to yourself to strive for love and peace in your heart. You will thank yourself for doing the work and the world will thank you for sharing.

As you see things coming true for you in life, please share them with me. I can't wait to see what greatness you bring into the world through your heart's desires. Post all of your wins online using #beanstalking or find me on social media so I can celebrate with you.

You have within you all that you need to make your life great. You are the director of your own play. You are the star of your own show. You get to pick the other characters, the plot, the setting, the props, the script, and the costumes. You can make it great, but don't forget to leave room for improv and a little magic to make it amazing!

Please leave with this note from me: There is no limit to your worth. There is no amount of money that could ever replace you; therefore, there is no limit to the amount of abundance, creativity, greatness, success, money, love, and happiness that you deserve—even if you don't believe you deserve it…yet! You are a unique and wonderful being and the world needs what you have to offer. Go be and do and live your best, most juicy life!

ACKNOWLEDGMENTS

I have so many people to thank for helping *The Beanstalk Book* come to be a real thing. Of course, the first is my husband in Heaven, Wes, for loving me so well, he showed me what loving myself would look like. He planted the original seed for the very first magic bean and without him none of this magic would be possible! I love him forever! I thank him for bringing so many magical things into my life while he was here and for all of the enchanting things he brought to me after he left...including Layton.

I also thank my husband on Earth, Layton, for tirelessly seeing me through the writing process and encouraging me through the rough patches. He is an amazing life companion, friend, and encourager. The healing we have done together is beyond my comprehension. I thank him for loving me through everything, and I love him forever!

My mom has been such a big fan of Layton and me when others struggled to accept us moving forward in love. I thank my mom for being terrific!

I thank my kids for making me proud and giving me courage to pursue my dreams so that I could model to them how to live their best lives and, more importantly, love their own selves first.

I thank my Magical Mentor, SARK, for the most amazing mentoring experience I could have ever dreamed of. Because of her, I have gotten two of my book ideas out of my head and into the world. I thank her for being an incredibly magical human! She showed me what I am capable of and gave me the tools to make great things happen in my life. I am filled with so much gratitude!

I thank Grace Kerina for being a wonderful, kind, and patient editor. She reminded me of so many grammar lessons I had forgotten.

I am grateful beyond words to Inger Kenobi and Sarah Bamford Seidelmann for creating the SHINE online artist salon and for each of the kind and loving members of the group. The support I have felt from this community of creatives got me through the hard parts of the publishing journey. They held me up when I needed it most!

I thank all of my students through all of my years of teaching, for making my life so rich, keeping my heart young, and for all that *they* taught *me* .

Thanks to all of my friends and family who encouraged and supported me through all parts of the journey in my life. Thanks to Jennifer Krupka-Sicoli and Rory Walkom for creating a safe and healing online space during COVID, and to Rory for translating messages from Spirit for me and giving me the words I needed to heal. They both have given me beautiful gifts.

Thank you to God and my spirit team, all of my angels and guides who are always here to help and support me.

Thanks to Treba Hollowel for telling me about "the invisible bag of gold" I was carrying. I think I finally found out what that means.

Thanks to my soul sister, Sheri Pope, for always understanding me, grieving alongside me, fiercely believing in me, and Beanstalking with me on Friday nights.

I am truly blessed to be surrounded by amazing people!

Thanks, also, to anyone who ever said to me, "You should write a book." Here it is.

ABOUT THE AUTHOR

Kim Nussbaum Howerton is a former elementary school teacher who lives in the mountains outside of Red Lodge, Montana with her husband, Layton Howerton, and their dog, Boone. They spend their time together watching sunsets and listening to the windchimes from the porch, exploring, reading, writing, creating music and art, contemplating the ways of the world and dreaming of their next adventure.

One of Kim's greatest joys in life is being a mother and grandmother! Alongside her art and writing, she is committed to helping others heal, grow, learn, and follow their hearts. She does individual and group help sessions. In this work she considers herself a heart coach and goes by the title "Your Fairy Godmother". She specializes in helping clients find the magic that already exists within themselves so they can realize their true potential and make their dream life their real life.